Wheeling Through Sand

Catherine Grant

malcolm down

PUBLISHING

First published 2026 by Malcolm Down Publishing Ltd
www.malcolmdown.co.uk

29 28 27 26   7 6 5 4 3 2 1

British Library Cataloguing in Publication Data
A catalogue record for this book is available from the British Library.

ISBN 978-1-917455-58-9

Cover design by Angela Selfe
Cover image painted by Phoebe Power

Printed in the UK

Prologue

I see there has been a storm, churning the sand and bathing the dunes with a wash of mineral-rich surf so that sanderlings, in a flock of speckled grey, frisk the grainy sand with bevelled beaks, not caring for my disturbance. Glistening sea kelp is scattered upon the beach like bedraggled green lizards sprawled upon a plateau left behind by the receding tide.

I climb the steps to a beach hut on a Dorset coast, turn the key in the door and step into my safe space. I raise every blind, and there is the sea. I fling open every skylight and unlock the door which overlooks the harbour, latching it back on a silver chain. Sunshine floods in. The air of early morning is fresh and cool, and from the lagoon comes the call of sandwich terns, screeching overhead as they take flight. In a few moments my favourite mug is set upon a tray and the kettle warms on the hob. My work table is placed across the open doorway, pens put ready, a pad of lined paper blank as yet, but waiting.

This will be the last day I will sit to write upon a page the things I have discovered about the life of my mother. I am glad there will be an end to it. My sisters were the catalysts who provoked this endeavour – but in truth we never were going to find the fairy tale ending they hoped for – or discover, along the way, an unexpected twist in the story to soften the account of Mabel's journey through life.

My mother was forty-eight when she died; I was fifteen. One of the most abiding memories I have is of a family outing to the seaside. I am ten. She is being dragged across the sand by strangers – lifeguards.

Balanced across the linked arms of reluctant teenagers, her skirt is riding high up her bare thighs and she is drooling, a white lace handkerchief held to her mouth with a shaky hand. She is laughing uncontrollably. Mabel is in the later stages of multiple sclerosis and at this time there's no treatment, and no hope of recovery.

There she sits in her wheelchair for many hours, in the heat of the day. My blind brother Clive is beside her on the beach; he is endlessly piling sand between his knees, sifting it through his fingers, gazing skyward, grinning at nothing in particular, rocking and swaying back and forth the whole day long. I have a photograph. Ladies sitting nearby in their cotton dresses and "kiss me quick" hats are pointing and staring. He is a curiosity for their entertainment.

Mabel Howe was born in a Somerset village in the 1920s, eloping with my father at the age of seventeen. She was a motherless girl searching for a place to belong and a person to belong to; he was a clever young man driven by reckless ambition, a dreamer of big dreams, a teller of stories.

I pour my tea, breathing in the glorious air of a Dorset coastline. The sun rises high over a cobalt sea; a gentle breeze kisses the fronds of marram grass upon the sand dune, a sparrow wafting here and there on its tip of green. I am rich indeed.

I pick up my pen to write – the final chapter and one, thankfully, of celebration. My life today is far from that of Mabel's – but I am still my mother's daughter; the baby for whom, my sisters tell me, she once saved sixpences in a jar.

PART ONE

The Scattering

1

Blagdon, Somerset, 2018

My sisters and I recognise the village our mother would have known a century before; pastures falling away on every side, ash trees in full leaf and the wild beauty of the valley stretching out below us under a wide, blue sky. From our vantage point here on The Mead we look out over a sweep of green bordered by lush hedgerows and, in the foreground and to our left, an ancient dry-stone wall; a nineteenth-century tessellation. Blagdon lake shimmers and sparkles in the early afternoon sunlight just a mile distant, and the faraway steeple of St Andrew's Church rises above a stand of oak trees.

At our feet, the grass of The Mead is worn thin and brown from the scrambling play of after-school children in summer; at our backs a row of pastel-painted cottages stand higgledy-piggledy, side by side near the lychgate. Tiny gardens explode with curated colour and a tortoiseshell cat is coiled upon a sunny windowsill, basking in the warmth of the day, copper coat gleaming gold and bronze. Beyond us and reaching out to the far horizon is the panorama that is the Chew Valley in all its summer glory.

Sarah, Joyce and I pause by the children's playground. It's here we come to remember our mother, a mother my sisters speak of with an affection I can't share. A mother I scarcely knew to be well, who died more than half a century ago. We set down our picnic baskets, crockery and flasks at the foot of the bench which bears her name on a bronze plaque.

"Beatrice Mabel Howe, 1921 – 1969."

"I wonder if we should have put brackets around the Beatrice." I'm thinking out loud. "She was never called that."

"Oh but it's such a lovely name!" older sister Sarah says. "And it's coming back!" She fusses over a posy of flowers wrapped in tissue. "Anyway, we must never put our mother in brackets."

Joyce takes a duster from her bag and polishes the inscription. Sarah has brought Sweet Williams, Mabel's favourite, and a length of red ribbon.

The Mead is deserted, school not yet out, and all around is held in a quiet stillness save for the rustling of trees and the whirr of a grasshopper's wing. A child's canvas shoe has been lost and found, thrust wrong side up upon a post, and a dog sends a deep-throated bark from a distant garden. The cat stirs, stretches, and settles herself once again. Sheep graze in the meadow beyond the wall, heads bowed to the ground, absorbed in the business of finding contentment. We tune out the rumble of the highway. All is peaceful, this glorious day in late summer; 25th July, our mother Mabel's birthday.

"I haven't remembered flowers for Grandmother Lily's grave." Sarah stands back to admire the posy of pink and crimson, set in scarlet tissue and laid carefully, for now, across the slats of the wooden bench. "We shall have to try at the shop. Our things will be safe here." A dedicated Bristol dweller, she adds, "It's not like living in the city, is it?"

We browse the shelves at the Blagdon Village Stores, a jumbled miscellany of groceries, hardware, sweets and stationery. A young woman in T-shirt and jeans is perched upon a stool behind the counter, absorbed in examining her nails. She glances up as we come in but doesn't smile. We are an inconvenience in a convenience store. A delivery of magazines tied about with string is set down just inside the doorway alongside tubs of multi-coloured jelly sweets, awaiting a moment when she might have a spare five minutes to put them on a shelf.

Bottles of milk in a grubby plastic crate warm nicely in the sunshine while the girl puzzles over a hangnail. A freezer, set against the far wall and stocked full of ready meals and frozen vegetables, rumbles and hisses in an effort to keep itself chilled.

"It's nothing like the Dainty's of the 1930s!" Joyce whispers, a little too loudly so the girl looks up from her filing but says nothing and her expression does not change. "Excuse me – have you had any fresh flowers in today?"

"I'm temp'ory," is the reply.

A green plastic bucket of tired flowers stands guard on the step; they sit in a dribble of murky water so I'm hopeful they will survive beyond this evening. It's no matter; the placing of the flowers is the most important thing. A nod to the past that my sisters feel is important.

We choose pink roses for our grandmother's grave and Sarah sees a Blagdon newsletter amongst the clutter on the counter – £1. The girl gets to her feet to serve us, huffing a little as she counts out our change, the calculation of £1.26 seeming too much trouble to be bothered with.

"Thank you!" Sarah says cheerily, though the girl does not deserve the courtesy. She perches herself back on the stool and takes up the nail file, hair falling across her face, and it is as though we were never there.

We cross to the lychgate, latching it behind us and heading down to the churchyard, retracing the Sunday morning steps of those three sisters of long ago.

"They certainly would have looked a picture! She used to talk about their white pinafores and hair ribbons!" Sarah is the oldest daughter who knew our mother far, far longer than I, the youngest.

"And running across the fields with Jane and Frances!" Joyce reminds us, picking up the pace to match our sister's generous stride. "She often told us stories about the fun they had together. Before their mother died."

I imagine those little sisters – they would be running, I'm sure, eager to be done with duty so that playtime could begin. Across The Mead and down, down the cinder path to St Andrew's, such a long way for little girls in sturdy black boots. Did they skip, giggle, race each other, I wonder? And was Jane, the eldest, bossy and impatient? Was Frances, little more than a toddler, annoyingly slow? And did our mother Mabel help her little sister as she struggled to keep up?

"Do you remember that awful story she told us?" Joyce asks Sarah as we stand aside, backs pressed to the wall as a lady with a double pushchair negotiates the path, "of the day they were late getting back from school, and Grampy's new housekeeper took the strap to them?"

"It's hard when a mother goes, and I don't think Stepmother Laura was much better. You can't replace a mother, just like that."

"I'm glad we've done the gravestone." Sarah stoops to place the pink roses gently upon the soil. "It's respectful, isn't it? To see their names written, there."

Reflections on the loss of a mother; I begin to feel the resistance that is "not wanting to know". The afternoon is going wrong. "Come on!" I say cheerfully, so we can side-step any more soul-searching, and turn to lead the way back to the path. "Let's go and have our tea. I've made a Victoria sponge, 'specially!"

"There wasn't any justice in her life," Sarah continues as if I haven't spoken, buttoning her jacket more closely at the neck. "And no one knows what she went through."

"Cath's the writer – we could tell her what we remember and she could write it all down," suggests Joyce brightly, as though I am not walking right there beside them. Older sisters organising the games for the youngest. It's always been so.

We weave through the kissing gate, one by one, and walk by way of the cinder path up, up across The Mead. The mood of the afternoon has changed. I'm in danger of being ambushed by a good idea. Confident it's simply the emotion of the moment, I decide that once I am home all will be as it was.

"If the three of us don't tell Mabel's story, she'll be forgotten for all time." Sarah is looking down at the ground as she walks.

"Let's go the long way round and go up to Glebe House," suggests Joyce, reinventing the light-heartedness, "It's always good to remember how happy she was there."

The High Street is just beyond the boundary of The Mead, the house where our mother spent her teenage years set on a grassy bank at the turn of the road. It's a solid, square house sitting in a country garden of roses and hollyhocks, white pebbledash freshly painted and windows sparkling in the July sun. It's good to see that it is loved still. A limestone rockery tumbles down to the pavement edge and clematis trails a wooden balcony that wraps around the front of the house. Marigolds mark the journey of the path from doorstep to grass verge.

"It's lovely to think of her in this house," says Sarah, her tone quite recovered from the bitterness of ten minutes before, "even though she had Stepmother Laura to contend with!"

"I wonder who lives here now. It looks well cared for."

We stand and stare for a minute or two but there isn't much more we can do so we make our way back to The Mead.

"So lovely it's a sunny day," I say, lifting us from the past to the present, "and we've supported the village shop, which is so important."

"Mum would be disappointed if she saw it now," comments Joyce. "It's so rundown."

And there it is again – a drift back into a history of sadness and loss we can do nothing to change, when this was never meant to be a day for regrets.

We reach our mother's bench. Here one sister spreads a rose-covered cloth, another sets out pretty cups and saucers, a third has brought tea. Sarah arranges the posy of Sweet Williams, secured with a bow of scarlet ribbon.

There is a birthday cake; it's our tea party for Mabel. An easy peace has been restored, for which I am grateful to Joyce and Glebe House combined.

A young mother passes by on her way to the school. She nods – perplexed, I think, to see the little tableau on The Mead.

"It's our mother's bench," I tell her. "She grew up in Blagdon. We believe she was happy here."

It's a beautifully serene summer evening, the motorway unusually quiet, and as I skirt the glorious rolling hills of the Marlborough Downs I catch sight of a gathering of fallow deer. Their coats of dappled red catch the glow of evening sunlight. I have passed through a gateway from the past to the present; from sisterly meanderings through an anxious and unresolved mystery of childhood to a future I have chosen all for myself. I decide that, all things considered, today has gone well. We've recognised our mother's birthday, when we never did in her lifetime. It's surprising we ever knew the date. We've relived some awful childhood times in our conversations together and declared ourselves glad they are over. We've remembered Mabel's love of Blagdon, visited her favourite house and shown respect to the memory of her mother. We've had a tea party at the bench which bears her name. A good day's work.

Dinner is ready to go in the oven at home, and tomorrow we board a ferry to the Channel Islands. It will be a happy chaos of cousins, all my children and their children piling into a house set upon the cliff top, a view of the seashore so we can check the tides and the surf before we plan our day. This world of family and togetherness is far more real to me than all the memories my sisters tell of a life long past. I remember very little of it – and care even less for remembering more.

Fifty miles to go and I turn the radio on for the news, catching the tail end of a documentary on an internet scam that has robbed thousands of unsuspecting people of their hard-earned savings.

"It was extremely clever in its marketing," the faceless presenter tells me, "calling itself 'I love you', and drawing people in because, of course, we all need to be loved!"

And quick as a flash, I speak aloud the words, "No we don't!"

Oh my goodness! There it is, spoken into the emptiness of my car. I press the off button and in the quietness of my own company I have to acknowledge the deepest of deep convictions, out of which I have very probably lived my entire life. The denial of the need of a mother. Of any need of mothering, since I have done very well at mothering myself. And I am deceived because, of course, that disembodied voice on the radio is absolutely right – we certainly do all need to be loved.

I've allowed my car to slow. Other drivers pass and I press my foot down hard to compete with their speed so I might not appear to be someone with no sense of purpose; no desire to be successful. Someone, perhaps, who might seem to be incapable of looking after themselves.

I pull into my drive a full hundred miles from the place where I was born and turn off the engine, sitting back for a moment in the quiet restfulness of my front garden. It is alive with pink roses and evening birdsong. A text from Sarah is waiting for me on my phone.

"Thanks for organising a lovely day. It's always lovely to visit Blagdon, isn't it? Our mother would be a hundred years old in a few years' time. Perhaps it's time to give her a voice."

2

Blagdon, 1931

When Mabel was nine years old, her mother died. Lily Howe tripped and fell, and she died. That's all the children knew.

The Waterworks cottage, set deep in the folds of Shoemaker Lane and once alive with young voices and the clattering of busy feet on wooden stairs, became a silent place. The four children crept through the house now, never running or bickering, reluctant to disturb their father for fear of provoking his sudden rages, a creeping blindness making him a feeble shadow of the man he once was.

Beatrice Mabel, sweet-faced and dimpled, eyes the colour of Prussian blue, was a child who loved nothing better than to lose herself in a book so she might enter a place of fantasy and wonder. She cared less for chores, much preferring to run free in the fields and meadows, seldom returning in time to help her sister put tea on the table, or hang sheets upon the line.

School was Mabel's delight, a place where mysteries of the wider world were solved and others of a more fairy tale nature could be fashioned with paper and pencil. There were dragons in her daydreams, of course, and handsome princes – but never a wicked stepmother or a captive princess. In the innocence of these earlier years there had been no need of rescue, no fear of abandonment. There never had been a more ordinary, everyday family; this new, motherless life was not the stuff of fairy tales, not at all. Rather it was a bleak and charmless landscape which had thrust them all into being people they did not choose to be.

3

Blagdon, 2019

We are at our mother's bench mid-morning on Monday, 18th May. I'd hoped the mission to write Mabel's story might have lost its appeal during these past months but today, as arranged by Sarah, we are meeting the lady who is a long-standing member of the Blagdon History Society. At the very least, I must put pen to paper and write the story of family life in the Blagdon of the 1930s.

It could be warmer – we are chilly souls and have all kept our coats on.

"Ne'er cast a clout till May is out!" Sarah reminds us, quoting a favourite adage of our mother's. She has an energy for the day ahead that I feel wary of – I am losing my place as the leader of all things Blagdon-related. She is sorting the tea while Joyce is doing her best to twist a length of garden twine around the stems of a bunch of Sweet Williams. The pink and scarlet posy, foliage a mossy green, is to sit upon the slats of the bench and bring a splash of colour to this corner of The Mead.

"They'll wonder why and read the plaque, won't they?" Sarah is fishing teabags from cups with a teaspoon. "When people pass the bench I mean. And they'll know that she's remembered."

"Hello, my dears!" I see an older lady approaching – I guess she must have come from one of the chocolate-box cottages that fringe The Mead.

"Good morning!" I move to one side of the path so she might pass, but it seems she is simply coming to say "hello" because she is still wearing her apron and carpet slippers.

"I've seen you here before, I think." Her plump face crinkles into a wide beam.

Joyce pauses in her efforts to keep the cluster of flowers upright while Sarah, always one to engage in conversation with older people, smiles and tells her, "We come as often as we can. It's our mother's bench."

"It's a lovely idea." The lady stops on the path, arms folded across her chest, leaning back a little as though settling in to chat awhile. "Did you all grow up in Blagdon, then?"

"Oh, no," I explain, "but our mother did – it's our parents' wedding anniversary today so we are celebrating!"

We aren't going to tell this lady that our thoughts and remembrances are all of Mabel, today, not him. We have agreed – it will never be about him.

"Well, I'll leave you to enjoy your tea," her voice is brisk but kindly. "And don't you worry about those flowers – I always come along and clear them away for you, once they're past their best."

"Oh, how very kind!" says Sarah with feeling. "That's so thoughtful of you. There's nothing more sad than dead flowers on a memorial!"

The woman waves a hand and turns away, still smiling.

"That's so good of her." Joyce gives up the battle to keep the posy upright on its thread of green. "Remind me to bring gaffer tape next time."

We have arranged to meet Shirley – she of the History Society – at Connie's Cafe, an understated gem at the end of the High Street, next door to the Village Club. She and Sarah have struck up an email conversation and Shirley has promised to help us delve through the archives. We seem to have officially begun our research into Mabel's life and my sisters have become animated by the whole scenario.

Racks of retro-style blouses, skirts and hats fashioned in tweeds and linen by Connie herself fill every corner of the tearoom, coat hangers identical and arranged in neat rows. A wicker basket of hand-knitted gloves rests upon the floor. Five pounds a pair. A solitary table of green Formica, a remnant of 1950s memorabilia, is placed beneath the window for customers. There are three wooden chairs with tapestry cushions of red and gold thread.

Connie is a lady of uncertain age, perhaps early forties, with an open, friendly face and a no-nonsense manner. When she asks us, "How are you all?" we know she will listen and care about the answer. She doesn't wear an apron so when we sit at the table in her little teashop it's like we've just been invited into her kitchen for a chat.

It's Sarah's turn to pay, so Joyce and I settle ourselves at the table. While our sister is sorting coffees and cake at the counter, chatting all the while, Joyce takes an envelope from her bag and passes it across to me.

"These are all the photos I have," she says. "There's none of us when we were a bit older – I think she couldn't use a camera by then, or probably the Brownie got left behind in one of our moves."

The photographs are all in monochrome. One is taken in a sunny garden, catching Mabel peeping round an open back door as John and I ride trikes up and down the path. We are dressed in khaki shorts and white shirts, plastic binoculars strung around our necks. My little brother is three or four years old, squinting into the glare of the sun as he looks round at his mother, and she wears a pretty floral pinny and is smiling back at him.

"I wonder who took this, then?"

"That's a good question." Joyce replies. "Perhaps she trusted Sarah with the precious camera."

I know each of these photos very well – we all do, so few remain from our childhoods to prove we were once young. That it all really happened. There is one of Joyce and me standing in the same garden in school gymslips and white cotton blouses, feet together, backs straight. Joyce has her arm around my shoulder, though I don't recall she was very nice to me when I was little so I'm guessing she was told to do it. Our hair is neatly brushed, my fringe cut straight as a dye with a circle of hair held back in a tortoiseshell slide. There are broiler chickens in the background, pecking at the bare earth.

"These are both taken at Eaton Bray," Joyce explains. "We didn't live in that house for more than a year or so, but I think she was really happy there. A village a bit like Blagdon and a tonic for her, I think, after the awfulness of the two houses we lived in before. You won't remember much of it, Cath – you were too young."

"I remember starting school," I correct her, "and walking to a park with John in the pushchair."

"I started Girl Guides there," she is a trifle wistful, "but I only went for two weeks because we couldn't afford the uniform."

Sarah takes off her coat, draping it over the back of the chair as she comes to sit with us. "I've brought the photograph of Clive." She opens her bag, "It's the one you had copied and framed for us, Cath." And I see she has cradled it carefully within the folds of a laundered tea towel. "It's the only one we have of him, isn't it."

Our blind brother is sitting on Weymouth beach, scooping sand into shapeless piles between bare knees. He is very thin with pale, angular wrists; his hair is cut short and stands on end, as though he has slept badly. It's a moment when I begin to join up the dots of our history – because, of course, he certainly would have slept badly, his bed at the time being a cast iron bathtub. Clive is wearing a shirt and tie, lace-up shoes and school shorts. Ladies in summer dresses sitting nearby are staring at him with unashamed curiosity. I search his face – as though after fifty years of looking, I will see something new there. He is smiling at nothing in particular. I wonder if we sat with him from time to time; if we joined him in his sifting of the sand. If we cared a little.

A few moments of silence are broken by Connie bringing a tray of coffee and teas. There are slices of walnut cake, Victoria sponge and chocolate flapjack. Joyce quickly moves the photos out of harm's way.

"Now, ladies, is there anything else I can get you?"

We smile and shake our heads, because now she has placed cups and plates and napkins on the table, there is no room at all for the "anything else".

"We're meeting Shirley in a minute," Sarah tells Connie, animated by the day she has organised, "so there will be more coffee needed in a little while."

"Oh, lovely! She's a regular here." Hands on hips, Connie is smiling broadly.

"Yes, we're trying to find out all we can about our mother's life here in Blagdon, that's why we're seeing Shirley. To pick her brains."

"Oh, well," replies Connie, "she's your man! If Shirley doesn't know about it, it probably didn't happen!"

Joyce takes a knife and slices each portion of cake into three equal parts, so we can all try a piece of everything. We are baker's daughters, after all.

The day has warmed up enough for us to sit outside, more customers coming into the teashop and there being but the one table. We step out onto the square of cobbles, Sarah putting her coat back on and setting a fourth chair at the table as we see a woman who must be Shirley coming from the Village Club and heading our way.

"Good morning!" she greets us. "How lovely to meet you all!" Her smile is genuine. She has a folder of paperwork under her arm. We introduce ourselves and she reaches to shake our hands, sitting down alongside Sarah. "I'm so interested to hear about your project."

Joyce pops back in to order more coffee and Sarah takes a handful of photographs from her bag, checking the table is clean and dry before setting them out for Shirley to see.

"This is the only photo we have of our mother in Blagdon, though we've seen a portrait of Lily and Harry Howe and their little family that was done a year or so before Lily died. Our cousin has the original."

Shirley picks up the photos one by one, taking care to handle just the corners. She rummages in the folder to find a newspaper cutting.

"Here we are," she says, "the Blagdon school photograph of 1932. Mabel and Jane are there, look – sitting together in the middle of the front row."

"Oh, how lovely!" Sarah is smiling. "They look so proud!"

"I wonder why they are wearing different to everybody else?" I ask.

19

Shirley shrugs. "There weren't really school uniforms in those days, but I should let you have details of Mr Jackson, the headmaster in the years after the First World War." She takes a sheet of text from her bag and hands it to Sarah. "Here – I've written it all down. He was a man with ideas way ahead of his time. He very much believed in the education of girls."

She is very interested in our plans to write about life in 1930s Blagdon and has already sent for archive material on our behalf – birth certificates, death certificates, census data. "Once a hundred years has passed, you can more or less get everything you want."

I pass back to Joyce the photograph of my little brother and me in the garden of a country cottage, taken in the days when we were too small to know the awfulness that was going on around us. I consider how John is squinting – perhaps even at this tender age he needed glasses, the blindness suffered by boys in our family coming through to the next generation, had we but known. I can remember the dress I am wearing very well – a soft cotton gingham. Yellow. It was my favourite, inherited from Joyce and much turned up at the hem. I can't, though, remember what was going through my mind when we stood so obediently still as my mother adjusted the camera and we heard the click of the shutter. The plastic binoculars remain strung about our necks. I'm smiling; perhaps it was a good day. Perhaps we were happy. Perhaps she said, "Smile!" and we did.

"We aren't quite sure of the dates our mother lived here in Blagdon," I tell Shirley. "We only know she eloped with our father when he was a conductor on the buses, and the crew used to come into her stepmother's teashop at Glebe House."

"Oh, yes! The bus was a great asset to the village, especially when the railway closed." Shirley tucks the newspaper cuttings back into the folder and hands it to Sarah. "It will be a pleasure to help. And as I say, so much material is available soon, a hundred years on."

"Gosh! A hundred years on." repeats Sarah. "We should mark that in some way, don't you think? We've talked about having a tea party on her birthday."

A trap is ready to close on me. "It was only a thought."

"An afternoon tea is certainly something the village would enjoy; the Village Club would be the place for that – I can introduce you to the secretary and help you with the invitation list."

I begin to stack cups and saucers, so we can help Connie in the clearing up. "It was only a thought," I repeat.

Shirley must go; she is needed elsewhere. "Keep in touch, ladies." She gathers her things, "And don't forget – I'll help in any way I can. It's only right that the stories of ordinary people are told. Because no one is truly ordinary, are they?" She looks up from her gathering of various belongings, and smiles. "We all have a story."

I was accustomed to setting off from our time in Blagdon feeling I had enabled a good day to happen, leaving my sisters with a sense of shared history and camaraderie. But since the notion of writing Mabel's story has become a certainty, and the responsibility handed fair and square to me, there is no peace of mind. And now, we seem to be planning some kind of commemoration on what would have been her hundredth birthday.

This is not just a fleeting idea any more – this re-visiting and writing of Mabel's history. It's become a living, breathing commitment, sisters excited and now even strangers involved and equally expectant. I sense the longing of my sisters for a happy ending; as though searching through the comings and goings of a family tossed here and there on the whim of a discontented and irresponsible father will bring some kind of satisfying closure. A resolution of all those bad things which happened to us. To our mother. To our brother. All those things we have no need of remembering.

"See you soon, then," Sarah says cheerily as I park at her gate. "Shirley is going to be such a help!"

Because we've lingered too long in Blagdon, the traffic on the ring road is horrendous. I shan't be home until well after ten o'clock. We have talked through a plan to visit the houses our family lived in; there are more than twenty, some now long gone. Sarah has already decided we should meet up with our cousin, to ask what he remembers about his parents' house in Bristol where Mabel and Frank began their life together in a rented room. A house where she was born and a second baby girl died in the wickedly cold winter of 1947; a house where Mabel heard of the death of her brother and had countless miscarriages, finding she'd escaped one acid tongue, her stepmother Laura's, only to live with another, that of her sister-in-law Doreen.

Our cousin will remember other things – things we know nothing of, as yet. It's important, I decide, as I turn onto the motorway and head for home, that we find something in that conversation to be glad about.

4

Blagdon, 1931

Less than six months after Lily Howe had been laid in the ground, Laura appeared. A diminutive, mousey figure, Laura Boylan had a face as thin as it was stern, plentiful freckles on paper-white flesh and watery blue eyes which blinked a good deal as she looked the girls up and down. Her eyelashes were so pale it looked to Mabel as though she had none at all. Thick, sandy-coloured hair was scraped back from a high forehead into a tight bun, secured with a thousand hairpins.

Mabel and Jane stood to attention in the parlour while she announced herself their new housekeeper, Father hesitating to interfere in the process of introductions but rather choosing to stand back and let the moment take its course.

"Florence Laura Dillon Boylan, mother deceased," she told the sisters, nodding like a sparrow as though to confirm the truth of it, the girls standing ramrod straight with hands clasped behind their backs, "and my dear father ex-Merchant Navy, so I like everything to be ship-shape and Bristol fashion!"

Young Mabel watched the woman's mouth move as she talked and knew this interloper must never, ever be allowed to take the place of their own dear mother. For Mother had been forever smiley, with sparkly blue eyes that crinkled at the edges when the tiniest thing amused her.

"Now get yourselves washed up for your supper," said Father, coming to life suddenly, "Miss Boylan's in charge now, so mind your manners!"

Once ensconced in the sisters' bedroom, the Waterworks' cottage having but two, Laura unpacked her valises and put her blouses in the wardrobe and her shoes in pairs beneath the chair. Her raincoat she hung upon the hook in the scullery, her galoshes she placed neatly beneath, heels together.

There was no time to be lost in creating order where there was none. Laura began work immediately breakfast was done the following morning, busying about the cottage to sort shelves and cupboards to suit herself, setting Jane to scrub the grease from the range and Mabel to take all the knick-knacks from the parlour and stash them away in the shed.

"No sense dusting what's got no use!" the woman said, testily, clicking her tongue and nodding vigorously as though in agreement with herself. The portrait of Lily Howe surrounded by her husband and little family she lifted from the parlour wall, where a square of dust forever reminded the sisters of its going. Laura carried it out to the old wheelbarrow so Mabel might transport it more easily to the shed.

They married, though it was little more than a year since Lily's death. Mabel, on an errand to Dainty's Stores, heard the woman behind the counter passing the time of day with a customer as she fashioned a pat of butter from the marble slab to wrap it in a fold of greaseproof.

"For what else is a widower to do but marry his housekeeper?" The woman's tone was melancholy, "And poor Lily and those two babbies not yet cold in their grave!"

Young Mabel, standing patiently in line and clutching two copper coins to buy Father's tobacco, saw the scorn and was mindful of a disgrace she could not fathom, running red-faced from the shop just as soon as her errand was done.

"But what did she *mean*," Mabel asked Jane as they undressed by the light of a candle, their bedroom a place of refuge once again now Laura had moved into their father's bed, "when she said 'the two babbies'? What did she *mean*?"

Jane took a hairbrush from the stool – they had no dressing table since Laura had insisted Father drag it from one bedroom to another – "It was the way of things." She began the hundred strokes of the brush Lily had always insisted upon. "You're too young to remember, but Mother couldn't always carry her babies."

Mabel climbed into bed, tucking her knees up tight. "It wasn't true, then, what they told us? That she fell and hit her head?"

After some moments, the only sound in the room the stroking of the brush, Jane snuffed out the candle between finger and thumb and climbed into bed beside her sister. "It's of no matter," she said, turning her back. "Dead is dead. Let's not talk about it anymore."

"I'll write," Jane assured Mabel, taking up her coat and latching the wardrobe door, all traces of her life in Blagdon packed into the bag their aunt had brought for her. "Every week. You know I will – not like brother Reg. Boys never keep in touch. And Frances is too young to write from Wales. Let's be sure to tell each other all our news. All the ups and downs."

Mabel nodded, wordless, running her hand across the counterpane on the bed, smoothing the wrinkles where Jane's bag had rested. "Write as soon as you get the chance, then . . ."

Laura called from downstairs. "The cart's here waiting! Don't be dawdling."

"Well, little sister, look after Father now – he can't see further than an arm's length these days . . . And don't you forget to send me all your news. You and I will always have lots to talk about!"

And Mabel promised she would; throughout all the coming years of separation. No matter if their fortunes might be so very different, she and Jane would share the ordinary stuff of life.

Jane took up her bag. "Because sisters are sisters, always," she said.

5

─────── ୭∘୧ ───────

The Channel Islands, 2019

Our holiday in Jersey has seen a mix of weather but no matter; it's a small cousins' paradise. They sail, they surf, they cycle, they skateboard. None of these words were ever a part of my mother's vocabulary, so I feel I've re-entered the 21st century, an altogether more comfortable place.

We collect an aquarium of "suckers" from a thousand sparkling rock pools, fashioning an undersea world with pebbles and saltwater and scraps of green seaweed in a plastic box. I insist we use a lid, though it provokes some concern about air circulation.

We enjoy a barbecue on the beach in a howling gale, hoods pulled up tight against the ferocity of the wind. Contrarily, though it takes an hour for the barbecue to warm through a sausage, it bursts into life when my husband holds it out the window at arm's length, the car climbing the cliff road home. It's a moment of cheering from the back seat and the one event the children all remember as being the most exciting.

We stumble over rocks, slithery with seaweed left stranded by an ebbing tide, and explore concrete bunkers and underground tunnels built by Russian prisoners of the Nazi occupation to deter the rescuing British – who never came – and explore Napoleonic towers of pink Jersey granite which defied the marauding French – who did. We cycle disused railway tracks, little ones pedalling free of all cares or thoughts of danger, my husband running along behind to scoop up casualties.

Family is family, and must be celebrated.

We are the most useful grandparents in the world, babysitting whilst parents go out for civilised meals in restaurants at the edge of the ocean, returning to a house quiet and settled for the night, the kitchen tidied and ready for the early morning scramble.

I am attempting to teach the little ones a few life skills, like picking up wet towels from the floor, switching off lights, flushing a toilet after themselves and leaving shoes in pairs – hopefully somewhere it might be possible for us to find them tomorrow.

"Look behind you!" I tell them a hundred times a day, but it's of no consequence. They aren't frightened enough of me to take much notice. I'm simply the wallpaper in their young lives, my devotion to each one of them taken for granted, just as it should be, their right to a place in our family assured; a testament to the everyday privilege of "belonging", about which nobody gives a second thought.

Summer holidays give way to returning home; to the necessity of school haircuts and shoe shopping, catching up with classmates so that the "first day back" might be a happy one, sorting the chaos of houses where children have run riot for nigh on two months.

We have one more week of sharing time with our youngest son before he and his wife return to California for their final year. Then I shall be back to my secret morning ritual, when I take his favourite cup from the shelf and say "Love you" out loud to myself, sitting to enjoy my first cup of tea of the day as though he is with me at the kitchen table and we are discussing the latest Test Match scores, or how my writing is coming along.

Today he has offered to come with me to the coast. I've discovered, online, there is a beach hut for sale on our most favourite stretch of Dorset sand. The huts, a quiet British Institution, rarely come on the market; more likely they are handed down from one generation to the next. There is to be a telephone auction and the hut will sell by Friday.

"Mum, you must be crazy!" It's not much of an encouragement from my youngest son, but I can see his point. We have driven two hours from home, parked up and walked a mile and a half in driving rain to look at a 1950s wooden hut on a sandspit that is unreachable by car. I'm dressed in waterproofs, a coat I once wore on a zodiac while exploring icebergs in the Antarctic, and sturdy hiking shoes. I am holding aloft an umbrella, fighting with a brisk north-easterly. He, a temporary Californian, is in jeans and trainers, no socks, a light anorak and a white baseball cap.

"I can't expect you to be impressed when it's such awful weather," I say, holding back from commenting on his choice of clothes. We are at last standing before the hut, an oversized "For Sale" board nailed to its front door. "But it will be lovely in summer."

"Mum, it's August," he replies, dolefully.

It's certainly very brown. The vendors have slapped patches of new paint here and there, probably to hide the rotten bits in the wood. Rocks and large pebbles plug holes around its base, the gaps a blessing for local mice looking for shelter and a free meal. Sheets of corrugated iron, also painted brown, have been nailed over the windows to protect the glass. The roof, mock tiles of 1950s green felt, sags in the middle. It is, after all, built on sand. I am reluctantly reminded of the biblical story. Brambles and marram grass fight for space around the front door, which clearly hasn't been opened for some time. A giant padlock secures a sturdy metal bar, as though valuable curios are stored within.

"How much did you say it was!" It's not a question.

"It's dual aspect, remember," I point out, quoting our newest best friend the estate agent.

We don't have a key so we have no choice but to simply trek back the way we came. We don't talk. Making use of the umbrella, I try to shield us both from the wind which, now we've turned around, is hurling a cold drizzle into our faces. To our left, the sea is grey and unfriendly; the Isle of Wight, just a mile or so distant, has disappeared into a rainstorm. To our right, should we dare to lift our heads into the squall to look, Christchurch harbour is a murky mix of low cloud and choppy waves. There's not another soul to be seen.

"You're crazy, Mum," he says again, his feet sodden, raindrops dripping from the peak of his cap.

I'm sorry our day together has turned out to be so very depressing. I buy him a bacon and egg sandwich at the Hikers' Cafe and he revives a little, but he is still not to be persuaded.

"We are buying it anyway," I say on the way back up the motorway, car windows fogged with the steaming of wet clothes, "I'm telling Dad to just close his eyes, switch off his brain and pay the money."

Little more than a year later, it's a wondrous thing. The brown hovel has gone, the new has come. Cladding as blue as a Caribbean sky, paintwork a glistening off-white Accoya. A wooden balcony, raised to overlook the sea, is a cheerful, no-nonsense pine which will bleach to a soft silver-grey, given time. The bottom step has already been reclaimed by sand. The hut now stands on half a dozen plinths of reinforced concrete.

The interior is a joyful mix of kittiwake blue and bursts of brilliant coral, as advised by my daughter. Summer sunshine sparkles in at the windows and just ten metres away the surf of an incoming tide spills onto a golden sand studded with glistening pebbles the colour of butterscotch.

"Wait until their first baby arrives," I tell my husband as we sit together with a glass of wine to watch the sunset over the serenity that is Christchurch harbour, "then he'll learn to love it."

"We still overpaid," he replies, ever the businessman.

6

Bristol, 2019

Shirley has given us the address where Mabel was in service as a scullery maid, and I've come to see it for myself.

The pretty wrought-iron gate stands closed but through it I see the sweep of a gravel drive edged in tiles of grey slate, a well-kept lawn, a shrubbery of azaleas and holly bushes. A double garage that might once have been stables. It is a gentleman's house, still.

I imagine fourteen-year-old Mabel walking around the back to the tradesman's entrance, brown suitcase gripped tightly in her hand. I wonder if she walked the three miles from the bus station, arriving breathless and dishevelled; thirsty. I wonder if her heart skipped a beat as she knocked at the door. I wonder, too, at her courage.

I text Sarah from the road where our mother learned to earn her own way in life. Where, perhaps, her imagination fashioned the possibility of new horizons for a girl with ambition.

"I can't possibly know everything that happened," I tell my sister. "I'm going to have to make it up."

"Oh, don't worry about that," the reply comes within the time it takes for me to start the engine, "she always lived in hope of being somebody different – somebody she could be proud of!"

And I recall our mother's "telephone voice", and know it to be true.

7

Blagdon, 1937 – 1939

Mabel had been summoned home from Bristol. Laura sent a note to Mrs Dawson – the Howe girl was required back in Blagdon. Any monies owed could be forwarded on.

Set high on a grassy bank at the bend in the road, Glebe House commanded a long view of the High Street. A wooden balcony in the fashion of Edwardian times, painted green, wrapped around the ground floor to the front door; a limestone rockery, edged in marigolds, tumbled down towards the path. Beyond the rear boundary lay the wide green fields of Somerset, set about with evergreen hedges and solitary oaks; to the left, a footpath skirted the next-door farm and led to . . . who knew where! It was all waiting to be explored and discovered. Mabel felt the possibility of adventure.

She climbed the steps, weaving her way through clumps of ox-eye daisies left to sprawl and stray. Moss grew unhindered between the stones and a young lilac tree, heavy with blossom, carried the scent of her childhood.

Her stepmother appeared at the front door, smiling and standing aside to welcome her in. "Good of the Dawsons to spare you," Laura said now, not ungraciously, closing the door behind Mabel and taking the small brown suitcase from her. It was an unexpected warmth of welcome.

Mabel followed the woman through the hall, an expanse of white emulsion, the vaulted ceiling with not one but two pendant lights, both with prettily scalloped shades, the staircase furnished with a crimson runner and an elegant turn of the bannister.

Laura halted for a moment to turn the brass handle of an oak door, throwing it open and nodding busily in Mabel's direction, eyes wide.

"This parlour will easily take ten or twelve tables," she said. "There's plenty of money to be made once we open the teashop – and plenty of spare bedrooms, once we're ready to take in lodgers."

Mabel began to suspect why she might be useful. She saw how easily she had been deceived.

Within the space of two weeks, the teashop became a reality, as her stepmother had determined. With Mabel on hand to set tables, clear the hearth, bake, bottle, peel, stew and cook, Laura was free to open the front door wide to customers, welcoming them in with the promise of free toasted teacakes on opening day and a more varied menu in the weeks to come. She was a busy person with plenty of excuses to keep her stepdaughter busier.

Once the board was hammered into place at the kerbside and the advertisement appeared in the *Western Daily Press*, men from the Waterworks and women from the local dairy called at the door to make enquiries. Rooms were let and rents collected in advance, men only too happy to share, older women less so.

No sooner was one meal taken from the stove and plated up, Mabel had need to turn her attention to the next. There was no let-up, no pause to write a letter to her sister or fashion a dress for Jane's wedding. Indeed, Laura doubted there would be time to attend, such was the success of the teashop and the boarding house combined.

There were plans afoot to change the living arrangements in the house. Mabel had seen the problem coming, but hadn't reckoned on her stepmother's solution.

Summer passed into winter, spring came upon the valley and war with Germany was only a matter of time.

The women of the village had grown accustomed to visiting the teashop on the High Street, such was the fascination of wiling away an hour, drinking tea and nibbling on a buttermilk scone.

"It makes a day of it," they said to Laura, she hobnobbing with the customers while Mabel waited on tables, going back and forth to the kitchen a hundred times a day to fetch this, bring that, pour the other. Settling back on mismatched wooden chairs in their Sunday-best coats, little fingers crooked as they sipped tea from Lily's dainty cups and saucers, the women looked for all the world like they were ladies of leisure and had not at all walked out on a thousand chores.

And when the crew of the Bristol Omnibus Services discovered the generosity of the portions, the extravagance of fruit cake wedges the size of a man's fist, they very often walked the few steps to Glebe House while the bus cooled its brakes at the kerb, the young conductor whistling the latest Ruby Murray or Ella Fitzgerald. And Laura was there at the door to smile and welcome them in, seating them at the best table near the window and personally bringing plates of Mabel's beef pie and onions, buttery mashed potato and rich, brown gravy. But it was Mabel who cleared their plates and offered steaming bowls of creamy rice pudding with generous dollops of plum jam.

As she later washed dishes and emptied teapots into a slop bucket, Mabel heard the rise and fall of the men's voices in lively conversation, the high-pitched tones of women who lingered to enjoy the novelty of grown men in a teashop, and wondered at the strangeness of it all.

"Get that lamb stew in the oven so we've plenty for tomorrow," Laura nudged Mabel to one side and tipped dirty cutlery into the washing-up bowl. "And when you've finished here, nip out and check that lavatory's respectable."

It became more natural, the waiting on tables where young men sat entertaining the ladies with stories of city life. The younger of the men, Frank, always had a joke to tell, or a compliment to offer, so that the local ladies sat back in their chairs and said, "Get on with you!", while their tea grew cold in the pot.

It was an easy deception and one which, over time, became commonplace. Deliciously reckless.

Sunday mornings brought Mabel a brief respite, Laura and Harry sleeping in after a night at the pub. Once the lodgers' beds were made, breakfasts cleared and the teashop set to rights after a busy Saturday, unless the weather turned wet or Frank couldn't borrow his brother's van, they were able to sit together for an hour or two on the old wrought-iron bench high up on The Mead, well away from the footpath and hidden from view by the low branches of a neglected ash tree. Precious moments of silent rebellion.

In the span of just a few months, Mabel's imaginings grew more real; a fairy tale took on flesh and blood. Sometimes as they sat together, she in her best dress and he in a collar and tie, they talked of nothing in particular; certainly nothing that mattered very much. Thoughts on the growing certainty of war, the preparations gathering pace in the city, the opportunities for Frank and his brothers now that other working men – those who were fit and able – were being called up.

"We all had TB as kids," he told her, the two of them seated one at each end of the bench on a bright and sunny morning in midsummer. "The Army won't want us, our breathing's too bad."

He told Mabel about his family; a bevy of sisters, two older brothers, parents who ran an off-licence and were fond of the demon drink. "I've seen too much of the damage it can do." His voice unusually serious, he lit a cigarette from a packet of five Woodbines and handed it to her before taking one himself, throwing the spent match onto the grass at their feet. "I rarely touch a drop, myself."

She liked that, his attitude to drink. "My father has a pint of brown ale now and again," she told him, so he might understand and appreciate their like-mindedness and admire her all the more for it.

"Our older brother Bert's the miserable one, but George and I do everything together." Frank gazed out across The Mead, crossing one leg over the other, leaning a little closer to her and resting an arm along the back of the bench so she felt the weight of it against her.

"He's married to Doreen and they've got their own house and two little 'uns."

"That sounds lovely!" answered Mabel, wistfully. "To be settled in one place, I mean. Not like me . . ." she allowed her voice to tail off, looking out beyond The Mead to where the blue of the midsummer sky met a distant horizon of green fields and faraway places. She felt the presence of his arm at her shoulder.

"You seem pretty well settled here," he answered, mildly, "with Laura and Harry." He looked sideways at her, flicking ash from his cigarette. "It's a pretty comfortable home."

"It's not my home," said Mabel firmly, wanting him to see the truth of who she was not, "Never has been since my mother died. It's Laura's house, bought with her money. I don't really and truly belong there."

Mabel studied the cigarette she held between her fingers, twirling the yellow bangle at her wrist. "It's not my home," she repeated, as though to herself. She would not tell him about the gurney in the shed, the rat scrabbling and scratching behind the flour sacks. She felt his eyes upon her. "A home has to be much more than just a place," she said, her voice scarcely more than a whisper. "For me, it's a destination. Somewhere I'm searching for."

Frank drew long and deep on his cigarette, the tip glowing red. He exhaled.

"I've got big plans," he said. "There are opportunities for a man like me; I've every intention of getting on in the world!"

Mabel sat quite still, looking out across The Mead where spiralling swallows dived and soared, strengthening their wings for the flight to come. "It must be a wonderful thing – to make your own way in life," she said. "To be your own master, at nobody's beck and call."

In the early hours of a September morning, when everything in Glebe House was silent and still, Mabel drew the battered suitcase from beneath the gurney and packed her few belongings with hands that trembled. She had very little – a pair of good boots, a cotton blouse sent to her by Aunt Annie, kept for Sunday-best, and a yellow bangle that had belonged to her mother, found by chance amongst an assortment of bric-a-brac Laura had banished to the shed. Last of all she took a precious package, tied about with string, that held together each and every letter Jane had written to her. And just the one photograph – unframed, a sepia portrait of a handsome, smiling young man. Mabel turned it over, her eyes resting for a quiet moment on the beautifully scripted words: "From your Frankie."

He had the most beautiful handwriting.

Mabel slipped the photograph into the little parcel of letters, there to be kept safe until she had a place to rest her head.

She snuffed out the candle and unlatched the shed door. There was a full moon, clouds chasing across its face in the chill of an autumn night. All was peaceful in the village, though not so Mabel's heart; she could feel the beat and thump of it in her head.

A breeze, fresh blown in across the meadows and unbreathed, as yet, by any other living soul, cooled her cheeks. She was free. Wonderfully free. To choose a life for herself, to become someone, to love and be loved. She came within a stone's throw of their rendezvous, boots soaked through and hair awry, fingers that gripped the suitcase numb from cold. She scanned the near horizon, faltering for a moment. He must come.

And he was there – waiting for her at the bench. A slight figure, shorter than she recalled, silhouetted against the velvety blackness of the sky.

He reached for her case, took her cold hand in his warm one and led her up, up through The Mead where she had once played and run, and run . . . a different life. A different Mabel. Now they were through the kissing gate, weathered hinge squeaking and groaning as they gained the road beyond, she stumbling on loose stones underfoot and Frank walking so very, very quickly, gripping her hand tight enough to stop the blood.

"Frank, can we go more slowly?" she gasped.

"Best get going before you're missed," he said gruffly, his voice different than she remembered. Younger. Less certain.

She was breathless, a stitch in her side and a brackish taste in her mouth from the rushing, though it might have been fear. Frank broke into a run, pulling her towards the waiting van.

"Get yourself up there, Mabe," he whispered hoarsely, opening the passenger door, "Let's be off. I'll just put this case through in the back."

Mabel grabbed it from him, clasping it tightly to her chest. "I'll keep it with me," she said. She climbed into the van and reached for the door so she might close it herself.

PART TWO

Settling – The Shape of Things

1

Somerset, 2019

I have a business engagement in Somerset so it's a perfect opportunity to follow up on Sarah's idea and meet with our cousin, younger son of George and Doreen. When I phone to say my sisters and I are coming to see him he is thrilled; in doing everything in my power to create kinship amongst the cousins of a new generation I neglect my own.

I collect Sarah and Joyce from Bristol on the way out to the coast twenty miles beyond the city centre. September has decided to mimic August, the day already bright and warm; traffic is light and the journey easy so we have time to waste before it's a respectable hour to meet up with our cousin.

"There must be a nice coffee shop somewhere in the town."

Joyce is ever the optimist because as we turn onto the Promenade it is deserted apart from an elderly lady in a brown coat walking an elderly dog. A figure – most likely a man – is hunkered down in a sleeping bag upon the slats of a bench in a Victorian seaside shelter, as though to prove that the passage of time has not prospered the lives of those who don't belong. He does not stir as I drive past, his head resting on a duffle bag; obviously the local council hasn't yet discovered how to replace a wooden bench with a row of red plastic seats – partitioned, so the unfortunate ones who have nowhere to rest their heads are kept from making themselves comfortable there.

The sea is to our left, the tideline a mile distant, this coast being famous for its mud, and instead of saltwater there is just an ocean of thick, brown sludge.

"I wonder if the donkeys are still giving rides for a shilling?" I speak with a touch of wistfulness because I remember happy times here; last-minute trips when, really, we children should all have been at home in bed. The consequence of a father who thought nothing through and did as he pleased, dragging his family behind him whether it was common sense or not. "I always chose the one called Prince."

"Oh, goodness!" exclaims my big sister from her seat in the back. "Did you really used to think the donkeys wore the same headband every time?"

Well, actually, I realise now, yes, I did. It's quite an adjustment in my thinking to believe it was otherwise. I feel a bit silly.

"You were only little," she says, her tone more gentle, "and half the time we were told stories, so how could you know fact from fiction? Do you remember he used to tell us the donkeys were given out to families to look after for the winter? And we always wanted one?"

And so the conversation ends with a shared moment of wry humour, and without acrimony.

It's a fifteen-minute drive to our cousin's – away from the seafront and all the nicer for it. He is so very glad to see us. His daughter makes us tea and we sit in the garden. My cousin is very like Frank: strong, broad hands, the same receding hairline, the same gangling, loping stride in spite of the passing years, the same chuckle in his voice and ready sense of humour, the engaging grin. But he is taller, more like his own father.

"Cath's writing our mother's story," Sarah explains as we enjoy our second cup of tea. "It would be Mabel's hundredth birthday in a couple of years and it seems right to show her some kind of respect, don't you think? Make her life seem significant."

I recall Shirley's words, "No-one is truly ordinary, are they?" and wonder if Sarah and Shirley have been in more regular contact than I had guessed. Nevertheless, I play the game my sisters have encouraged me to begin and I tell him we are finding out as much as we can about our mother's life in the years before we were old enough to remember.

"We don't know anything about the time they lived with you, during the war, when they were first married. None of those things were talked about in our family, so we can't know."

He offers around a plate of biscuits his daughter has set upon the table. A small white dog with a blue leather collar comes to say hello. He lifts it onto his lap and it turns and turns about before settling to sleep with a long and contented sigh.

"Auntie Mabel and Uncle Frank lived with us for three or four years. Maybe five. They rented an upstairs room. I was quite small, but I remember Frank and my father were thick as thieves!" Here he grins, reminding me of the boyish young man he used to be. "Always up to some scheme or other, the two of them. Pit ponies they bought cheap because it turned out they'd only walk backwards in the shafts, black-market trading during the war years, wheeling and dealing down the vegetable market and then losing it all down the dog track! And the Bristol Blitz, of course, the fear when the doodlebugs came over – all of us hiding under the kitchen table till the 'all clear' was sounded! It's quite an adventure when you're a small boy." He pauses, "They all rubbed along well enough, though our dads were always in trouble with Doreen about the trips to the bookies!" He leans forward to pour more tea. "You were born in Wootten Crescent, Sarah, and your little sister Carol shortly afterwards . . . she was tiny. Your aunt Jane came the morning she died, I remember."

Sarah nods, and I see from her face this is dangerous ground. "The bad winter of 1947, 'The Big Freeze' it was called. It started snowing in January and didn't stop till March!"

"I know we all had whooping cough . . ." He takes a spoonful of sugar and stirs his tea, "Uncle Frank sat up all night with the two of you, but Baby Carol was dead by morning – she was so small, you see."

"Yes, I remember Auntie Jane coming. She wheeled the pram out to the shed." Sarah is picturing it – the empty pram, the parlour curtains drawn in a 1940s morbid respect for the dead, the face of our mother.

"I wasn't allowed at the funeral, children weren't in those days. But Laura and Harry went, and I know they came back for tea afterwards. Auntie Doreen made sandwiches and Auntie Jane came on the bus and brought cake, and we sat in the best room with the fire lit and plates on our laps."

"And of course," our cousin continues, "as you can imagine, Doreen and Stepmother Laura had plenty to say about it once Jane left for home and your mother's back was turned! Laura made it very clear what she thought about all those babies lost or born too early. And Doreen was happy to listen – she'd seen too many miscarriages not to believe it!"

I'm sure we sisters are each thinking the same – if only our young mother had been surrounded by sisterly love, and not sharp-tongued judgement.

Our cousin lifts the little dog onto the floor at his feet. He picks white fur from his trousers. "Well, it was all a long time ago," he says philosophically. "There might not have been social media back then, but there was no shortage of rumour and guesswork!"

The dog whines, affronted. He bends to tickle its chin. "And they certainly lost a good few babies." It is an afterthought; a nothing.

I bring to mind my lovely daughter suffering the agony of baby loss and try to imagine Mabel's struggle managing a 1940s miscarriage on the floor of an outside toilet. Or worse.

He reaches to take a biscuit. "I remember Laura told us in no uncertain terms what the family thought was happening." The little dog, sure of its place in the world, jumps back onto his lap and he offers a corner of biscuit. "That your mother Mabel got rid of her babies."

There are long moments of silence. I hear Sarah's sharp intake of breath. Joyce is staring into space as though she cannot believe what she has just heard. The air is drenched in angry and unspoken words. A shroud of misunderstanding and shame separates us, as always, from the world of "Respectability".

I put my teacup down as carefully as I can. I'm thinking of my two little granddaughters, loved and wanted and precious, cradled in shawls of feather-stitch; tiny bonnets of delicate, white filigree. My daughter's face, a tortured mix of the deepest love and the loneliest grief. The tiny coffins. I feel the clenched fist of injustice in my stomach; an overwhelming urge to fight back.

It is the moment when Mabel's story begins to be mine.

2

Bristol, 1945 – 1955

Married five years and still lodging in George and Doreen's spare bedroom, Mabel knew they had outstayed their welcome long ago. When the letter arrived offering Frank a council house she didn't care that it was second rate or that it stood in a shabby road at the back end of a rundown housing estate; she sent Frank to the pillar box to accept by return of post.

Frank turned the key in the latch of the house in Lowden Road and Mabel followed him in, holding tight to little Sarah's hand. The floors were bare, windows grimy with soot and the exhaled smoke of a thousand Woodbines. Walls of faded green distemper were pockmarked here and there by the careless placing of chairs. Every ceiling had been stripped of lightbulbs, brown flexes hanging, redundant, so flicking the switch gave no welcome light.

Stepping through from one room to the next, Mabel saw that damp crept along the skirtings, black mould speckled the back wall and though the freshness of an early summer morning might have brought some relief, the windows were sealed shut with layer upon layer of lumpy brown paint. The scullery, set at the back of the house and reached by means of a dark and dingy passageway, had barely enough space for a table and chairs – although, as Mabel reminded herself, they had no chairs. A single, leaky tap dripped into a stone sink, pitted and stained a murky grey with age and neglect.

"It's going to be hard to make this place homely, Frankie," she said, her voice kept light, wary of seeming ungrateful. "It could do with a bit of attention – now that distemper's off the ration." She pulled her coat more closely to her. "And it's colder inside than out! We'd best order in some coal and light a few fires to air the place."

"It could certainly do with a bit of fresh air in here!" he agreed, his tone jaunty, coming to open the door to the back yard. He shot the rusty bolt across and rattled the brass knob without success. Peering through the dirty pane, he used his elbow to rub clean a circle of glass. "The privy's out there and that Anderson'll come in handy for storage. I'll sort this door first thing in the morning."

"What about using the lavatory?"

"I've got a bucket in the van. I'll go and unload our stuff and you can make us a cup of tea. Doreen gave us some milk."

"I'll bet she did!" Mabel said under her breath.

She let Sarah run off after her father while she stood, hands in coat pockets, stooping a little to get a better look through the window into the back yard. It was a scrambled mess of weeds bordered by a wayward hedge and bramble bushes. In time, there might be blackberries to make jam. And somewhere safe for Sarah to play. And for the baby that she suspected was on the way, if all went well – a place to set the pram beneath an apple tree.

"Bring the food boxes through, Frank," she called, "and buy some lightbulbs while you're out!" She heard the front door slam. Taking a pinny from her bag, she put it on over her coat.

Joyce was born in early November. There had been other babies – babies who did not make it past the middle months, babies who could not be thought of or imagined or planned for, their safety so uncertain; but this little girl was, as her name suggested, a joy. Golden curls and a sunny disposition. Mabel cut down a sheet for cot linen and unpicked her best cardigan to knit up a matinee jacket, bonnet and leggings. "Make do and mend" was still the order of the day, the country in the grip of rationing though "Victory" had, according to Clement Attlee, been won.

No matter that money was short, that comforts were scarce, that children demanded every ounce of energy she had. Though she protested, though she pleaded, though she tried reason, Frank would not be dissuaded. By March she was in the family way again. Her only shameful thought was that this one, like so many others, might be lost.

Mabel's labour pains began in the early hours of the morning in late August. She could tell Frank was scared. Too early for a baby to be well, but too late to manage the disaster at home as they'd done so many times in the past.

"Frank, you mustn't stay," she told him as he helped her down from the van and rang the emergency bell at the hospital entrance. "Leave me as soon as you can and get back to the children." She was past hoping the pains would stop and all would be well. "I'm sure I shall be home tomorrow, one way or the other."

He grunted, supporting her with a strong arm beneath her elbow as she took off her coat and leant against the cold red brick of the wall. Footsteps sounded, a blessed sign of help coming. A light came on inside the building. The awfulness would soon be over and she was grateful for that. She closed her eyes for a moment against a wave of pain that stopped her taking a breath.

"They won't let me stay, anyway, Mabe, I'll wait till they take you in and come back in the morning."

It was very soon done, the scrap of life coming into the world with little pushing required. A stranger in a green overall and face mask whisked the baby away.

"What is it?" Mabel asked, her voice hoarse, but no answer was forthcoming. She feared the worst and closed her eyes as the room blurred around her and the voices of the people, who had not yet asked her name, faded. All she could hear was the rustling of starched skirts and, from the corridor outside, the shrill ringing of a telephone. She could not hear a baby's cries.

3

Bristol, 2020

We meet at Joyce's house and I drive the five or six miles to Lowden Road. It's a fascination to me that my sisters still live so very close to where they grew up – no one in my town has the least idea of where I came from or who I used to be – or what I ran from. I have reinvented myself without any complication of shared memories or shameful family secrets. I am free of all that – until I write it upon a page and the world gets to hear about it, and a written truth will betray me.

It's a gloomy, overcast day in late February, not conducive to a cheerful outing and just eighteen months before the mythical Birthday Tea in Blagdon that my sisters are so excited about. I feel we are running out of time to visit each of Mabel's homes before her centenary; perhaps it was an unrealistic plan.

I park at the kerb outside the house that was our mother's first proper home, my car noticeably newer than anything else nearby. I don't believe we should step out, though the rain has held off. Better it remains part fiction – the reimagining of our mother's heartache in this place, seventy years before.

Boxy, semi-detached pre-war houses – front doors each painted a different colour though not all of the cheerful kind – in private ownership since the 1990s' "Right to buy". Front gardens have generally been converted into hard-standing for cars, dropped kerbs breaking the symmetry at either side of the road. Green plastic wheelie-bins, facing every which way, stand randomly here and there, abandoned by early morning binmen. Litter flutters from one pavement to another. All is quiet; deserted. No children play hopscotch in the road, neighbours don't cross to chat to a friend across the street, no one has planted flowers along the length of a front path or set their empties, glass washed clean, in regimented lines upon a step, a note left in the bottle for the milkman so he leaves an extra pint.

I open the window of the car and look out on the house where Mabel endeavoured to make their first home. A house where Frank promised her a new beginning, but never gave up his old ways.

"That's the door she opened to the telegram boy, the morning she heard Uncle Reg had been killed," Sarah says. "It's one of the things I most remember about living here – the sound of her screaming."

"He was driving, wasn't he?" Joyce glances back at her sister. "And probably had the eye problem."

"Oh, no," I too-quickly correct her. "Retinoschisis is x-linked recessive – carried by the mother and presenting in fifty per cent of boys. Grampy couldn't have passed it onto Uncle Reg, only to his own daughters."

I start the car. I don't want to pursue this conversation because I am the fortunate one; the sister with sons unscathed by genetic imperfection. "Let's drive to the hospital the way she would have gone on the bus to visit Clive."

"I hope I behaved myself when she had to take me on that bus three or four times a day," Joyce muses. "I was only nine months old!"

"Oh well, you were never the one in trouble." Sarah is sitting back in her seat, glad to go, I think. "You were our father's favourite, remember!" There is no edge to her voice – we are sisters together; loyalty is never in question.

Joyce giggles, not one to hold a grudge. And anyway, we all know it to be true.

I turn the car in the road and head down the hill towards the hospital where our mother's first son was born.

Prematurity is the thread which connects Mabel's story of motherhood with that of the next generation, and the next. I'm praying that medical science has halted its progress – though it hasn't done so yet. Disability is the thread which unites us as a family, the impact on a life only present in the eyes of the beholder.

I have a nephew – he is brave and good-hearted and has learnt courage. He has a wife and children who respect him, grandchildren regularly in and out of his house and a technical skill which takes him to Europe on business. He is registered as "Severely Sight Impaired", but would never consider himself to be disabled; perhaps he would rather the prejudice he meets were redefined as "misjudgement", an interpretation of difference founded on ignorance. Misplaced and unnecessary pity.

When his sister is dangerously ill he visits her in hospital, wandering in a blur of finding his way through one department after another, this way and that down one dimly lit corridor to the next until his wanderings take him through a door marked "Restricted Area", the sign written in small print, indented grey lettering on black. Alarms ring. Security guards are called. He is escorted from the building, one man on each arm.

He weathers pitying remarks from well-wishers who have no idea of his past struggles, or the success he has fought so hard to win. He has put behind him teenage years of rebellion – truancy, foster care, detention centres, court rooms – and has become a philanthropist with both his time and his skills.

He has forgiven the fates which handed down an injustice he did not deserve. He didn't run, as I did, but rather he found the courage and resourcefulness to reinvent his future right where he was. I am so very proud of him.

He has studied for a Bachelor of Science degree in computer coding. We go to his graduation in central London and clap till our hands hurt.

4

Bedfordshire, 2012

The labour ward is tense, the doctors scarcely speaking, so determined are they to deliver a baby who might yet prove science wrong. I feel a leap of joy as I hear his cry – the tiny whimper that is my grandson's voice, this scrap of wonder, twenty-four weeks and five days' gestation. It is a sign of life that we dared to pray we would hear – and then he is gone, whisked away by steady hands while my daughter is left, scarcely knowing she has become a mother because, once again, her baby has been taken from her.

They bring me a chair of red faux-leather. I sit in a dimly lit green-tiled passageway – there are no windows – opposite the door to the room where babies struggle to be strong. A porthole allows me a glimpse of life beyond. Now and then the door swings open as professionals come and go and I crane my neck to see the farthest crib, over near the window, where my little grandson lies shrouded by tubes and machinery and charts which tell his story. I see my daughter bending over him, her hand pressed gently upon the dome which warms and protects her little son.

I have been that nurse for other daughters' babies. I trust I smiled often, gave them hope perhaps or, at the very least, the comfort of knowing that I touched their little one with loving and gentle hands when they could not, that I whispered sweet words as I shocked their tiny bodies with heel pricks and sudden movements, the tubes sustaining life harsh and sharp against transparent skin. I trust I called their babies by name, proof of who they were and who they might become.

We learn to love this NICU; for three months it is our world. We come to admire their commitment, trust their belief in the preciousness of life and find comfort in their quiet empathy. Because now I see my daughter's face and it is changed from the girl she once was, and she has come to tell me the latest news – so up and down, even hour by hour. It can never be the definite promise of goodness that we are longing for, because the life of my little grandson, 650 grams of miraculous grace, hangs by a gossamer thread and relies on the skill and bravery of strangers.

My sisters arrive – a surprise visit. We drink tea, they explain they have come from Bristol by train, bus and then taxi. We haven't been together in this town since the days of our childhood, a place where our own mother climbed the stairs on her hands and knees.

They stay an hour. I make tea from the miscellany of teapot, cups and milk my daughter and I have assembled on the windowsill of Sideroom F over past days, and we chat about this and that. We don't refer to tests or results or medications. Outcomes. We only listen as my daughter describes how beautifully formed he is, how very proud she and her husband are to have a little son, how they came to choose his name; how very kind and clever the staff are. Sarah and Joyce smile and nod and tell her how very wonderful it is. How they can't wait to meet him. They leave to make the five-hour return journey home. Aunties are important – and we are sisters together, always.

Three weeks in, there is a small moment of triumph.

"His nipples are forming!" My daughter describes the spark of excitement she felt as she witnessed the hitherto secret world of life in utero. "His breast milk's been increased, too," she sits beside me on a plastic chair in the corridor to take the sandwich I put together in the early hours of the morning, "0.6 millilitres an hour down his tube. I'll express again when I've eaten this."

The expressing room is little more than a large cupboard beside a noticeboard which displays pictures of babies who have overcome the odds and gone home. Some of the photographs have been pinned to the board for a very long time, colours and contours of infant faces faded and blurred.

There are days when I sit for many hours in that corridor, using an iPad to send messages to family and friends who hold that little family in their prayers. A friend and colleague, J.John, an internationally respected preacher, is speaking at a conference in a cathedral. "We all spent a moment in prayer last evening," he writes. "A thousand people. God is good." I want to believe it's true.

My face is very familiar now to the staff who pass me by and smile their hellos, my daughter forever through the door in that secret place where miracles might happen. But here she is, and I rise from my chair to suggest we find a cup of tea and sit together somewhere different for a few minutes.

We leave the unit by way of heavy rubber doors, pressing the security buzzer to be let out, passing a couple who are coming through the doors the other way, she, slightly stooped, in a dressing gown, her partner with a hand beneath her elbow. They are so very young, but their faces are aged with worry and exhaustion – the same weariness I see etched on my son-in-law's face when he comes straight from work to meet us, always fearful of what the day has brought and what the news might be. And my daughter does not acknowledge this couple with even a nod of recognition, though she stands near their baby's crib for hours at a time, day after day. Because in this world of "anything might happen", no one wants to share the bad news of others, or, alarmingly so, the good.

We cross the tarmac to the main hospital building, thankful for our jackets in the chill of an April afternoon. A light rain has been falling and the air is crisp and clear on our faces, the sky china blue and freshly washed. We had forgotten that spring had come. There are no flowerbeds here, or trees, or shrubberies. We walk through tiled corridors to the cafeteria, a place where people come and go and chat about nothing in particular. We sit on white plastic chairs at a white plastic table, and my daughter tells me her little one is to have an R.O.P. test. "To make sure the oxygen isn't damaging his retinas," she explains. And I think of my brother, Clive, and remember the injustice; wonder if, after all, he wasn't born with the familial retinoschisis, for that comes on slowly and steadily. No, it was most probably the life-giving oxygen that robbed him of his sight, the less than gentle handling that caused his epilepsy. The prevailing attitude that caused him to be forever thought a nuisance.

We buy another cup of tea, served to us in cardboard cups. I'm brought back to the present because my daughter reminds me we must go; she cannot be away from NICU a minute longer. The doctors are due and we must return, me to my vigil on the chair and my darling girl to push through that swing door which divides fearful mothers and their fragile babies from the world of Happy Families.

And here I am, Mabel's daughter, mothering the mother of a born-too-early baby, holding onto hope while carrying in my heart the heavy weight of uncertainty – sharing the fear of what might yet come upon us. Because it's less than six months after the grief of a baby girl lost, one awfulness pressing down upon another with no space in between so our hearts might recover.

I visit the toilet and lock the door, sitting for a while blessedly out of sight of the comings and goings of others. I phone my friend Sue. She answers immediately and I love her for demonstrating that I am surely just a moment away from her thoughts.

"I don't think I can do this again."

I drive home, past ten o'clock and both of us exhausted by a day of waiting, watching, fearing to guess at what might be the end of our story. To dwell on one day at a time – this is all we allow ourselves. We are later than is usual and I know my little family will have cobbled together some kind of dinner for themselves. My teenage son has exams, though I've lost track of which ones and when. I know from the lateness of the hour and my daughter's face there has been a long discussion with her favourite doctor about treatment. If I wait long enough she will tell me.

The motorway is strangely deserted, lights along the central reservation illuminate the carriageways on either side; a steady rain sparkles in the yellow glow. We never tune into the radio, news of the wider world an irrelevance.

"He may be going for his heart op. tomorrow." My daughter is slumped in her seat, hands quietly folded in her lap. "Great Ormond Street have a bed in ICU."

It's my training hospital. I imagine it – the busyness, the sense of purpose, the professionalism of a Centre of Excellence. I miss it. I miss being part of a team that believes it has all the answers.

"Good. You've been waiting for that news." I keep my voice level, not wanting to encourage too much hope because, ultimately, I cannot be sure.

"Yes." Her voice is flat and tuneless as though we are discussing the weather. "They take him on a blue light. It's tricky transferring him onto a mobile ventilator for the journey. Takes about two hours."

I know she will have asked all the minute details; my daughter, a First Class maths graduate, has needed to become an amateur medic. "Will you both be able to stay?"

"Yes. They're giving us a room across the road from the hospital."

"Good." I speak with emphasis because I love that we can share that word; it's such a rare thing and I let it hang, for a while, in the space between us. "Which unit is he going into?"

She tells me. Though my time on staff is over, we have found other ways of supporting the work of my training hospital. The unit she speaks of is the one to which our Family Trust donated a sizeable sum two years before. Before we knew about life in NICU.

"It's only been open a week," she says. "He will be one of their very first patients."

It's thanks enough, and in a world where I am clutching at straws I decide it's a sign that God has gone before us; a reward for "paying it forward".

"Will he come back here once the heart op. is done?"

"Oh yes. If it's successful," she tells me in the same level tone. "There's always a risk of a brain bleed when the babies are moved." We sit without speaking for a minute or two and I think again of my brother Clive. I indicate and take the slip road and we are four miles from home. "It'll be nice for you to spend a few days in London."

There is no respite from the roller-coaster that is the NICU ride. Staying to watch the struggle is torture – or perhaps it is more true to say that staying to watch the torture is a struggle. Consenting to treatments that cause pain and fear is like a knife through a mother's heart. But going home, mixing with the world – that is far, far more unravelling. We don't belong in the world of the normal, not for the present. Best we remain living at this pitch of fear and dread so the next time we career into the pit of despair it is not so very far to fall.

5

Bristol, 1949

Past seven o'clock and the girls were at last settled – nine-month-old Joyce in her cot and five-year-old Sarah in bed though not yet asleep, her head full of Enid Blyton imaginings, playing dolls beneath the blankets; a tent fashioned for princesses and Happy Ever Afters.

Frank was finishing his dinner, fork scraping the last vestiges of mince and gravy from his plate. He'd had a difficult day with his brother – Mabel heard the whole story from start to finish as she piled dirty plates and saucepans into the sink, wiping her hands on a wet tea towel and filling the kettle from the tap so she could make Frank a fresh cup of tea before she left for the hospital. Third time today, and the bus due in less than twenty minutes.

Frank bent to pick up his paper from beneath the chair, sitting back and crossing his legs. The kettle sang on the hob as she wiped the draining board and scoured the bowl. She hung the tea towel across the back of a chair, warmed the pot, spooned in the tealeaves and poured the water. Outside, a steady drizzle spattered the kitchen window. The hole in the toe of her shoe meant she would need to slip a plastic bag over her foot before she ventured out tonight. She dried the saucepans and set them on the shelf above the cooker.

"Are you still up and out at four tomorrow, then?" Apron put ready so she could pick it up as soon as she came back, Mabel poured the tea and set the cup in front of him. She took his empty plate to the sink. "For the fruit market?"

He sighed heavily, opening the *Evening Post* at the sports pages and flicking the broadsheet into some kind of manageable shape. "Nope! George can get on and do it by himself for all I care."

Mabel saw the conversation was over. "I'm off then – with milk for the baby." She took up the shopping bag from the sideboard where she'd kept it safe from small hands. "I'll be an hour or so, depending on the buses." He could so easily have offered to drive her, the children perfectly safe to leave for ten minutes.

"Please yourself," Frank replied from behind the newspaper. "I'm not sure why you bother. They told you – he'll never be right."

Mabel took her court shoes from the under-stairs cupboard. She walked the darkness of the passage to the front door, taking care to set the bag safely upon the bottom stair before lifting her coat from the bannister. She called up the stairs as loudly as she dared, "Get to sleep now, Sarah, school tomorrow. Don't forget to go to the toilet and be careful not to wake your sister!" She unlatched the door, cloth bag over her arm, and took the path to the street.

Lowden Road was empty of life, it being the lull between tea and bedtime. A single street lamp shed a murky glow upon bins set here and there on the pavement ready for dustbin day tomorrow. As she stepped from the kerb a paperboy on a pushbike flashed across her path and she drew breath, coming to her senses and looking more carefully to the left and right as she crossed. She must be quite invisible to the world, a weary woman in a brown tweed coat with unkempt hair and snagged stockings, shopping bag on her arm, going who-knows-where at this time of night. She'd purposely not glanced in the hallstand mirror on her way to the front door.

Mabel picked up the pace as she headed down the slope towards the main road, each council house she passed identical to her own, some gardens tended, others not. And at number 34 the familiar bevy of unwashed milk bottles littered the doorstep, a roll of sodden newspapers delivered long ago tucked in behind; a black umbrella, part furled, left to mould against the doorframe, stowed there on a rainy day many months before. Blackout blinds at the window were pulled down against the scrutiny of the world. A wartime Vera Lynn number was playing, volume turned up so Mabel could hear the words of the refrain. In all the years she had lived in this road, she had never seen the old lady who lived here; rumour had it a young son had been lost in the Bristol Blitz of '39.

Mabel's footsteps were the only sound in the empty street aside from the yapping of a small dog somewhere close by and the rumble of traffic in the near distance. Tap, tap, tap, because the heel of Mabel's shoe was worn through and the metal cap exposed. She'd forgotten the plastic bag; her feet were sodden.

She took a headscarf from her pocket to cover her hair, tucking stray curls beneath so she might look half presentable for the hospital. She sidestepped dustbins, some with metal lids half cocked in an overflow of meat wrappers and old cabbage leaves, holding her breath as she passed pig-bins uncovered and set askew, raided by vagrant mongrels and sharp-eyed pigeons, lamb bones rustled and stripped of goodness to be left in gutters or at the fringe of a nearby privet. Their own dustbin, she remembered, was round the back. Frank would not think to put it out.

Mabel shrugged the bag up onto her shoulder and turned the corner, glad to reach the brighter street lights of the main road. Low cloud had brought a chill not expected on a late August evening and she wished she'd picked up a cardigan. She pressed her hands deep into her coat pockets for warmth, fingered the coins she found there and was grateful because her purse, she realised now, was left upon the sideboard. Doubtless the ten shilling note from this week's Family Allowance would be gone by morning. Mabel quickened her step, reaching the bus stop just as the number 8 came round the corner. She put out her hand.

Settling herself into the softness of the moquette for a precious few moments of rest, Mabel watched rivulets of condensation meander down the window, the cloth bag safely upon her lap. It weighed nothing at all.

"Hospital!" sang the conductor, and Mabel took up her bag and alighted, holding the rail so she would not stumble in the dark. She walked the length of the hospital drive, stepping to one side to avoid those who had been visiting family and friends. Some were chattering together – relieved to hear good news, perhaps. Others, faces caught in the half light of a street lamp, seemed lost in thought. A few were walking the driveway alone, as Mabel was.

She crossed to a low outbuilding of grey breezeblock, innocuous in its ordinariness; but within – this was where miracles could happen. Mabel pushed through the heavy swing doors to a brightly lit corridor beyond, air heavy with carbolic soap and antiseptic. Rubber doors slapped closed behind her. A concrete floor was painted grey – there were no windows. Empty cribs lined the walls on either side, some with a sheet upon a rubber mattress, some without. Whether languishing there in hope of new occupants or in memory of lost ones, Mabel could not guess. There was no sound in the world that lay beyond those rubber doors. She walked the length of the corridor, an intruder in this place of experts; her shoes tap-tapped her progress, a regular rhythm like a heartbeat. A door opened at the far end.

"Why, here you are again!"

Of middle years and as neat as a pin in a navy-blue uniform and crisp white apron and cap, the Special Care Sister looked Mabel up and down as they met halfway, the woman a human barrier between babies and mothers. "You're here very late!"

It was not said kindly. Mabel felt her face grow hot, the humiliation of a circumstance she could not name – her shoddy appearance perhaps, the shame of birthing a baby too early, her own pointless to-ing and fro-ing to nurture a scrap of life not worth the effort of caring. She reached up to take the scarf from her head, thrusting it into her pocket as rainwater dripped onto the floor.

"What can I do for you at this late hour?" Sister made a point of checking the fob watch fastened to her apron by a silver chain.

Mabel forced a smile, opening the bag to rummage, fingers fumbling from cold. She unfolded the shroud of tea towel and offered the jam jar. It was still warm – an intentional offering of comfort to a baby she had never held. "My milk, for the baby," she said tentatively. "I'm sorry it's so late . . ."

Her face impassive, the Sister did not respond so Mabel blundered on, hopeful that all was well but nervous to ask. "How is he tonight? Has he had a good afternoon? The doctors were coming, I think?"

The woman stepped forward to take the jar, holding it gingerly between forefinger and thumb so Mabel feared the lid would give way and the precious contents spilled. "Yes, Doctor came," she answered in a level tone, successfully giving no sign of comfort or false hope. "Baby's much the same. We've increased his oxygen, to try and improve his colour."

"Thank you." Mabel did not know if this were good news or bad. "Might I go in to see him?" She knew what the answer would be but asked anyway.

"No, we don't like our babies to be disturbed." The Sister turned away to resume her busyness. "It unsettles them." She took a few steps and looked back at Mabel, considering her for a second or two before continuing, "Probably best you come in without that toddler tomorrow. We like to keep disturbance out of the unit, you see." Then she was gone, through the door to the room where mothers were never to go.

Mabel walked to the bus stop, the streets deserted and a few hopefuls standing in line at the side of the road, grey-faced, some with evening newspapers tucked under their arms. The buses were running late again, then, it was ever so since the days of the war. An older gentleman in a brown macintosh and tweed cap shuffled up so Mabel could stand under the roof of the shelter and she nodded "thank you", looking into the near distance, as others did, to watch.

Her feet were soaked through, the soles of her court shoes no match for the puddles in the darkness of the pavements. She felt the rub of wet leather on a blister at her heel.

Even if she thought really hard, reliving those frantic minutes in the van and then the chaos of a labour ward woken from its sleep, Mabel could not recall what her baby's face looked like, the smell of him or the sound of his cry. She thought now, as she stood shivering at the bus stop in the half light of evening, that if ever she were allowed to walk into that hallowed place beyond the door, she would need to check the names on each and every cot so she might discover which baby was hers. They would be strangers, she and him. She knew only that he was a boy and she had named him Clive, her breasts and the bleeding the only reminder that she had borne a child.

The hospital chaplain had been summoned to the Unit by Sister, there to make the sign of the cross upon the baby's forehead while Mabel was stitched and washed, and in the rush of things she could not recall now if she had given the child's middle name as Frank or Harry.

6

Bristol, 1952

There were endless clinic and hospital appointments, assessments by nurses, interviews with a woman from the Social Work department and examinations by doctors of varying abilities, the last of whom wore a suit and tie in place of the white coats Mabel had grown accustomed to.

"Lay the baby on the couch and hold him very still," he said, whereupon he took an instrument from the trolley, using the contraption, which seemed to Mabel to have come from the Middle Ages, to prise the toddler's eyes wide open and hold them there. While little Clive struggled and moaned, the expert leaned in close, a magnifying glass fitted with a bright light. The child did not flinch with the intensity of the light but writhed and struggled, angered by the force of his mother's arm across his chest. In his world of darkness the menace had come at him without warning.

The letter from Bristol Eye Hospital informed her that "The Authorities" would be in touch in due course.

The woman, of late middle age, steely grey hair cut short and dressed in a dark suit and white blouse buttoned to the neck, knocked on the door at 2pm precisely, as indicated in the letter from the Bristol Education Department. A pearly brooch was her only adornment, pinned slightly askew on the lapel of her jacket.

"Good afternoon." She looked past Mabel to the passageway beyond. "I'm Miss Goodwin. I've come to see Clive."

Mabel stood aside, a black and white collie pulling his mistress over the threshold.

"The sitting room is to the right," she told the visitor, unprepared for this first meeting with a person from the world of the unsighted. "Shall I make tea?"

With a stuttering "Let me show you in . . ." Mabel closed the door and side-stepped the dog to take the woman's arm briefly, so she might guide her to the settee. Feeling the cushion behind her knees Miss Goodwin perched, rather stiffly, on the edge of the seat. She reached down to unclip the dog's harness so the animal could run free.

"Is young Clive here?"

"He's having an afternoon sleep," Mabel lied. She climbed the stairs to get the child. It had been easier to leave him in the confines of the cot while she scurried around to tidy up for the expected visit. Had she known the woman had no sight, she need not have taken the trouble.

She reached into the cot, Clive not raising his hands to be lifted; rather he was startled by his mother's sudden appearance. "Come on," she said, "let's do our best."

Miss Goodwin took a set of plastic tumblers from her shopping bag. The multicoloured cups nestled one inside another, like a Russian doll.

"Here's Clive," Mabel said unnecessarily, at a loss to know how and when and to what extent to paint a picture of a world the woman could not see. "Miss Goodwin has come to visit us," she said to the boy, as though it were a perfectly natural, everyday occurrence for her to explain circumstances to the child.

As Mabel placed Clive upon the floor between them, Miss Goodwin reached down to put the cups in front of him. She scattered them so he began to reach out, his attention caught by the sound of plastic rolling across Lino.

"Can he stack these?" she asked. "It's something we look for – coordination and dexterity."

"He has his own toys, of course," Mabel answered, though it was an exaggeration. "His sisters play with him a lot. After school." She moved the cups closer to the boy with her foot – quietly, so the woman would not guess she had helped. Mabel saw the dog was making himself at home, sniffing at the fringed edges of the hearth rug before setting off to explore the downstairs.

"Does he take himself to the toilet?"

"Yes." She did not say that his father forbade any visits to the toilet after bedtime – that the child wet himself frequently and his clothes were dried, as they were, on the fireguard, and put back on.

"Can he feed himself?"

"Yes." Mabel did not elaborate, did not explain that Frank insisted the boy sat alone to eat so the mess and waywardness of food shuffled around and off the side of the plate with a spoon might not irritate his father. And if anything were to be left on the plate, it would be put in front of the boy again at the next mealtime.

The dog came back from scouting around Mabel's kitchen floor to lick Clive generously on the face, whining and wagging his tail all the while, and the boy giggled with pleasure, reaching up to run his hand through the softness of the dog's fur, squirming his legs in excitement at the novelty. Mabel smiled to see it.

"He's never seen a dog before," she said, then was conscious of the flaw in the sentiment.

Miss Goodwin seemed unfazed. "I'll be your Home Visitor from now on," she said, gazing across the room at nothing in particular, which Mabel found disconcerting, "so we can assess him and decide what's best to do with him."

"Of course." Mabel twisted the yellow bangle at her wrist, nervously wondering how to answer – what was right to say and what was wrong. "Do you want to see his reports from the Eye Hospital?"

"No need," the woman replied. "We have copies."

It was the moment when Mabel guessed; saw there were conversations and decisions which had happened – and indeed were still happening – that she knew nothing of and about which she could voice no opinion.

The world of "the handicapped" allowed no interference from those in the world of "the normal".

They sat in silence for a few moments. Clive took a cup in each hand, knocking them together, swaying a little back and forth as he sat cross-legged upon the floor, head circling as he considered the shapes of the plastic toys. He had no intention of stacking them, rather he lobbed one across the room, turning his ear to the place where it fell. The dog scampered to investigate.

"How often does he fit?"

"Once or twice a week," answered Mabel, wary of judgement now she realised the weight given to the answers; the influence of this woman over what happened next. "We're used to managing it."

Clive had tired of playing with the cups. He got up from the floor and toddled forwards, falling over the visitor's feet and pitching into her lap so Miss Goodwin jumped, startled by the unexpected. She clutched at her bag.

"Oh goodness, I'm so sorry! Here – let me take him out of your way." Mabel stood to lift the child. "Can I make you a cup of tea?"

"No, I must go." The woman got to her feet, straightening her skirt, feeling for her white stick and picking it up. "My driver is waiting outside." She reached for the armrest of the settee to get her bearings. "Now, where is that dog . . . ?"

Mabel saw it was behind the settee, cocking its leg.

"What are they after, then?" asked Frank when Mabel described the woman's visit. Busy reading the *Evening Post* at the kitchen table, he spoke without lifting his eyes from the page.

"I think they might be checking up on us." Mabel wiped down the draining board with a wet cloth and untied the apron from her waist. "Perhaps this Miss Goodwin's assessing him for the Bristol Blind School."

"Well there's nowhere else for him!" replied Frank, turning to the sports pages and flicking the broadsheet into shape so it was easier to handle. "He can't be put anywhere normal."

"I told her he fits a lot," persisted Mabel, though she saw he was already studying the form for tomorrow's race card. "She said a lot of the children do. She wanted to know was he taking phenobarbitone yet." It rolled off the tongue, this strange word from the world of medications. It sounded expensive; she trusted it would come on prescription courtesy of the new National Health Service. "Miss Goodwin's going to look into it. She's sending me another appointment."

"Well," said Frank, irritably, "that might be the answer then. Let the authorities sort him out."

It was the end of the matter; he went back to his racing tips. Mabel left him to it and went to check on the children. She found Joyce sitting cross-legged upon the floor in the front room, teaching Clive the colours of each cup by size so that next time the Home Visitor came her brother would impress with his cleverness.

Miss Goodwin had news for Mabel when she called again; she had found Clive a place at the Sunshine Nursery for blind children. It was residential. "You've done the right thing," the woman assured her, taking back the form Mabel had signed and returning it to her bag. She sat up tall and straight, neat as a pin on the settee, drinking tea from Mabel's best cup and saucer whilst her dog wandered. "It's all for the best – for the boy to be with his own kind."

Now three children were registered to them and the sharing of bedrooms by boys and girls frowned upon, the council offered to rehouse them into a larger place and out of the blue they were given a house set on the edge of the estate and backing onto open fields. Frank and Mabel took their little family and their few bits of furniture and moved around the corner to a house filled with sunshine and light in a quiet cul-de-sac, painted cream with gardens front and back.

7

Bristol, 1952

Two days after the move, though Mabel asked her husband more than once to move the pile of boxes in the passageway, or clear the back door of rubbish he had jettisoned from the van, or perhaps give some thought to asking his brother George for more hours in the greengrocery shop to boost his wages, Frank decided to set to work on the front garden.

Mabel came to the front door, teacloth in hand, hoping there might be a lull in his commitment so she might again remind him of the chaos within. The morning sun was warm on her face and she understood why Frank had been tempted into the garden.

Shirt sleeves rolled above the elbows, old flannel trousers caught at the ankle with bicycle clips and boots bought from the Army and Navy, her husband looked as though he meant business. Using a garden fork, presumably borrowed from his brother's shed since they had never bought one of their own, Frank was turning the earth along the length of the path. Breaking up the clods and forking them through, he sifted out stones left by careless builders and tossed them into the hedge.

"Frank, I could do with a hand in here," she said, as amiably as she could. "I know it's lovely weather and you want to make the most of it, but I have to go up the school to register the girls and I really wanted help to empty the last of these boxes before I tidy myself up to go."

"George told me he's got a contact down the flower market," he said without looking up, "so I'll get this soil ready to plant out and then I'm off down to St Nick's market."

And off he went, gone for over an hour though Mabel knew he had seen her struggling to make a way through the downstairs passage, children pestering for their dinner so that Mabel needed to give up on the unpacking to search for plates and cutlery in the shambles that was the kitchen.

"Mummy, we would *love* to take a picnic over the fields!" pleaded Joyce in her most plaintive voice, tossing blond curls, "*Please* can we?"

Mabel regretted her shortness of temper. "Get a box then," she told the child, "and I'll fill it with whatever I can find – I haven't got much bread."

"And can we take a blanket, Mummy," Joyce persisted, "in case the grass is prickly?"

"And some lemonade," chimed in Sarah. "We need lemonade, that always makes it seem like a real picnic. Like in *Famous Five*."

By the time Mabel had sorted the girls, Frank was back with the van. She'd got nothing done at all apart from emptying cartons and jars from random boxes, now spilled out all over the table.

She kept the annoyance from her voice as she went to call from the front step. "How did you get on, Frank?" He was unloading wooden boxes of seedlings and two sacks of what she guessed to be horse manure, the earthy smell reminiscent of her mother's vegetable garden in Blagdon after a shower of rain. "Shall I bring you a cup of tea?"

Frank looked up for a second or two, raised his eyebrows and waved a "yes", intent on his task of reinvention. "Just wait till you see this once I've finished. It'll be a picture!" He slammed shut the door of the van and began to place the boxes of plants here and there along the length of the path.

She watched for some minutes, enjoying the blessing of an afternoon sun. She saw her husband's determination to please her, the care with which he was placing each root of marigolds, each clump of Sweet Williams, her favourite. He had brought a box of leafy snapdragons from the market, and now he was measuring the gaps between with a wooden rule borrowed from Sarah's pencil case, diligently spacing the roots equidistant along the inner edge of the privet. Mabel felt the beginnings of a new fondness. She smiled, leaning her shoulder on the door jamb, and Frank looked up and caught her eye and grinned. She was reminded of how boyish he had seemed, back in the days when their cares had been so much less complicated.

"I'll put the kettle on."

Joyce pushed past her skirts to help her daddy play with the mud. "Can I do some digging, Daddy?"

He handed her a trowel. "The red-headed woman over the road called by this morning and said she'd come to say a proper hello about now." It was said casually, as though it were of no consequence, Frank bending his back to the task of rooting out a clump of dandelions. "Don't be long with that tea, mind, this is thirsty work!"

Mabel sidestepped the stack of boxes yet to be unpacked, scooped Frank's donkey jacket from where he had flung it across the bannister and, in the absence of any coat hooks, folded it neatly across the back of a kitchen chair. She should have insisted on her husband smartening himself up as he worked away in such a public space because, really, that old shirt and trousers were a disgrace.

She stooped to pick up a cigarette butt from the kitchen floor, slipping it into the pocket of her skirt. She would salvage the tobacco later. She put the kettle on to boil – not for Frank's tea, now forgotten in the worry of being visited, but to tackle the washing-up left scattered across the draining board. She took yesterday's newspaper from the table and an empty teacup of slops from the windowsill. She rummaged in a box of linen for a clean tea towel and hung it, symmetrically, on the oven door. Taking the broom, she swept mud from the kitchen floor across the threshold and out into the back garden, closing the door after it so a visitor might not see the haphazard collection of crates and boxes discarded there, evidence of a job half done.

"Get upstairs and find a hairbrush," she ordered Sarah, the girl sitting quietly at the table, hair falling across her face, absorbed in a Nancy Drew adventure she had read many times before. "Now!" Mabel emphasised when the child didn't move, "and bring me down a cardigan for your sister. A nice one."

"But, Mummy," Sarah's forehead puckered in a frown, "I've just got to the exciting bit!"

"Get yourself upstairs and don't answer back!" said Mabel sharply, so the girl scrambled to her feet. Mabel picked up the offending book, adding it to a pile of papers and brown envelopes. She opened the nearest drawer and stuffed it all out of sight. The jars and packets of food she had rummaged from boxes were still in disarray across the worktop. She took the kettle from the hob and a clean rag from the cupboard under the sink and set to work on the dishes from the night before. She sprinkled the sink with Vim and scoured it clean of tea stains.

"Mummy!" Joyce called through from the front door. "The lady across the road came over!"

Mabel turned off the tap and fumbled with the straps of her apron.

"She can't stop now," continued Joyce. "She said she might call in tomorrow."

A week or so into their new life and Mabel set off to the shops – some distance away but a nice enough walk with the little girls trotting beside her. She bought blue Basildon Bond notepaper and matching envelopes from the post office, walking back without the inconvenience of meeting any of the neighbours and still in plenty of time to peel potatoes for Frank's dinner, so that it would be ready on the table for when he woke from his afternoon sleep. A slip of paper was caught half in, half out of the letterbox.

"Sorry to miss you," Mabel read. "Be sure to come and knock at my door, number 32, when you have a minute to spare." It was signed "Kay".

While the girls explored the back garden and found their own fun in the wilderness there, Mabel put potatoes on to boil and settled herself at the kitchen table to write to Jane so she might let her sister know their new address.

"It's a lovely house," she wrote in her neatest hand, "and the children are so happy here. There's a big garden for them to play in, and fields over the back where it's safe for them to explore. They've already had a picnic! Do you remember, when we were little, we used to run across the fields in Blagdon in the days when we still had Mother, and not give a thought to the time until we were hungry enough to go home!"

She stopped, her pen poised above the paper.

"I'd love you to come and see it all. Everything's brand new – the kitchen, the flooring, the outside toilet, and Frank's making such a lovely job of the garden. It's the prettiest in the road. And May is such a lovely time of year to plant it out."

She paused, glancing out of the open door to the scrubby expanse of garden where the raised voices of her girls told her there was disagreement brewing. Sarah wanted one game and Joyce another; it was ever so, Mabel smiled to herself, with sisters. She saw that the empty packing crates were still strewn about the back path and was reminded of her neighbour.

"There's a mother just down the road that's already called in to say hello," she turned the page and adjusted the line guide beneath the paper. "I've been invited over for a cup of tea as soon as I can make the time. And the lady next door is such a lovely woman, always a kind word for the children. She used to be a nurse, I think. We talked over the back fence just after we moved here and she's asked us all in, next month, to watch the Coronation. She has a television set!"

She did not have any news of the latest W.I. meeting, or the church jumble sale, or the bargains to be had at the drapers. There was no interesting gossip to report about the goings-on in the street, or a recent charabanc trip to the seaside – not like Jane's letters.

She finished off with a simple "Hoping to hear from you soon, love Mabe." She put down her pen, folding the pages of her letter carefully and neatly, sliding them into the envelope and securing the flap.

She licked the stamp and placed it in the corner, writing the address halfway down the page just as Mr Jackson had taught them.

There was no news given of Clive; the sending away of the child had long troubled her sister. Tomorrow she would write a quick note to the authorities and tell them of their new address. No hurry. She'd been told Clive had settled well enough at the nursery; all in good time they could have him home for the weekend. Now she would send Sarah to the pillar box with the letter – it was only on the next corner – and it would catch the afternoon post.

The girls' shouts were gaining momentum and Mabel must call them in for their tea. She had whipped up batter for pancakes, letting it stand an hour or two so it might be made all the lighter, and the pot of strawberry jam she'd bought on their trip to the shops would be a nice surprise. The potatoes came to the boil and began to spit and splash onto the hob.

Mabel stood to stretch her legs, not prepared for the shock of pain that ripped through her body, the cramping of her insides, the fall to the floor, the rush of warmth between her thighs. She cried out as her shoulder cracked beneath her, calling for Frank to "Come quick!", eyes tight shut against the griping wrench of pain. She doubled up, as though she herself were a baby in the womb.

"Mummy! Mummy, what's happened?"

Mabel opened her eyes, and all she could see was the scarlet offence of blood seeping onto the Lino, colouring her bare thighs with a jagged crimson. She could hear a child screaming, the spit of a saucepan boiling over on the stove, the thump of Frank's feet coming down the stairs. Closing her eyes, Mabel turned her face to the floor.

"Get upstairs, you kids," came Frank's voice. "Don't come down till I call you."

8

Bristol, 2019

Because of my sisters' descriptions of our mother's favourite house I have a picture of a spacious, sunny road, perhaps with trees and pretty garden gates. But as we approach Bradley Close I see it's quite insignificant, a narrow road set behind a parade of mediocre shops.

"Those shops weren't built when we lived here," says Joyce. "It was quite a way to the ones on Fulton Avenue with us walking and you in the pram. It took us ages."

The road is of no length at all, sloping upwards with the house we have come to see set to one side at the top of the cul-de-sac. The pebble dash is a muddy brown, the curtains at the windows a dull grey net. A front path, once planted out by a young husband trying to please his wife and arrayed with all her favourite flowers, is now bordered by tufts of overgrown grass and dandelions, the gate left open and leaning to one side.

"I suppose the front garden might look a lot prettier in summer," Sarah suggests apologetically.

"That was Mrs Hardy's house, that one with the red door!" Joyce points out the car window. "We were never allowed in, but Mum often went over there for a cup of tea."

"And there's Mrs Newson's," says Sarah, "next door to us, where I told you we went to watch the Coronation because they were the only family in the road with a television. It looks just the same!"

Perhaps memory is kind to us when we reminisce, because the house needs a fresh coat of paint and new windows. Perhaps in the 1950s, rationing scarcely over, all houses looked rundown and dreary.

"Except the front garden's gone," Sarah continues. "The world's full of cars now, isn't it?"

"Do you remember," chimes in Joyce, "we sat on the floor near the television, and all the grown-ups were crammed in on chairs they brought themselves? We had orange squash."

"That was such a special day!" says Sarah, whimsically, conveniently forgetting that sitting cross-legged on the floor in silence for three hours was tantamount to a punishment. "And everyone dressed up to the nines for the occasion! We had new hair ribbons, and white cotton socks, I remember, and Frank wore a suit and tie . . ."

"But remember, though," Joyce butts in, ever the cheerful realist, "that was the night they had that terrible row, and we heard them shouting so we hid under the blankets until it went quiet."

"Nothing unusual about that, then! Whenever she thought she was having a good day, he made sure he did something to spoil it."

"Remember I'm a Coronation baby," I say, wondering now if I was conceived more in a moment of violence than anything which might be considered "love".

Sarah buckles her seatbelt, ready to go. "They were excited about having you," she leans forward a little, over the back of my seat. "They saved all their sixpences in a jar by the front door."

I find I'm smiling. Imagine that. After all the trauma and sadness of babies dying and babies lost and babies born too early, my mother had the fortitude and resilience to begin again. I intend to hold that truth in my mind and count it as a moment of connection. Of mothering.

Joyce takes her phone to get a picture of the house as I start the car. "I still have fond memories of living here, even though it was sometimes horrible, because of the rows."

"It was because of Mrs Hardy she loved it here – having a friend. She'd never had one before," Sarah's voice is quiet. "That's what made the difference. And she never ever had one again."

"I have a friend who is special. She thinks nothing of calling at the door uninvited," I tell my sisters as we leave this place of happiness and struggle and head back to Joyce's. "Just like Kay Hardy was to our mother. I call her the friend who teaches me what 'fun' is and she calls me the sister she never had."

It is just three days after my daughter's first baby, a little girl, has died. We sit together in our house, a quiet place, set apart, for now, from the wider world. Sympathy won't help, and empathy is impossible for anyone who has not held the tiny form of a beautiful and perfect baby who is warm, but does not breathe.

"I'm not stopping," Sue reassures me as I open the back door, "but I didn't know what I could do, so I brought you these." She hands me a box of tissues. It is the perfect gift in the midst of the most imperfect of circumstances.

Now, in this very place where the story of baby loss played out two generations before, I remind myself once again that I should have told them. I am a paediatric nurse and health visitor, after all. I should have caused a fuss and not stopped causing a fuss until they listened, those professionals who told my daughter all was well. Because I knew. I knew but had chosen not to know – to disregard; to forget. Babies in our family come early; babies are lost. It's an indiscriminate inheritance passed down from a mother who died so very long ago; an ordinary woman with an extraordinary disability.

"It's an unusual problem," the consultant told me as we discussed how and when my second baby would be delivered. "Commonplace in the West Country, in the triangle between Bristol, Bridgewater and Bath."

Which is, of course, exactly where Blagdon is.

9

Bristol, 1953

"I'm going to Mrs Hardy's for a cup of tea after school today," she told Frank the Monday morning after the Coronation, as though it were the most natural thing in the world and she did it every day. She put his breakfast in front of him and he looked up from reading the sports pages.

"You don't want to get too pally with the neighbours," he warned. "They get to know all your business."

"I don't have any business," Mabel assured him. "Anyway, I think it will be lovely for the girls – I think she has two about the same age."

Frank sniffed, cutting into his rasher of bacon and dipping the forkful into a perfectly fried egg. "All I'm saying is, don't get too friendly." He squirted a hefty pool of brown sauce onto the edge of his plate. "I'm late back tonight, I'm meeting George at Eastville. He's got wind of a sure thing."

Mabel chose her words carefully, taking plates and bowls from the shelf and measuring porridge oats into a pan of milk. "The rent's due Friday," she struck a match to light the gas. "Let's not get too far behind."

Half past three, the girls collected from school and busy at the kitchen table with colouring pencils, Mabel went straight upstairs to change her dress for something less dowdy. She stood before the mirror to check the suitability of it. Though the skirt was full and rather flattering it was tight around the bodice, her waist more stout than before she'd had the children. She hoped to goodness she wasn't in the family way again. No need to worry about that now; a corset, though of a great age, would help.

The cotton dress, cherry red with white polka dots, showed her slim arms to advantage. A black petersham belt gave it structure. Taking her best shoes from the floor of the wardrobe she dabbed a spot of pink nail polish on the run in her stocking. She would need to cross her legs to hide it. She patted her hair into some kind of shape, regretting she had used the last of the shampoo on the children. Sunlight soap had robbed hers of any lustre it might have had and yes – Mabel stooped to peer more closely into the dressing table mirror – there were one or two grey hairs appearing at her temple. She tweaked them out with a wince of pinprick pain. Taking the pad from a tiny cardboard pot of rouge, Mabel dabbed colour onto each cheek, turning this way and that so she might be assured of its uniformity. She applied the lightest touch of red lipstick, describing the corners of her lips, most carefully, with the end of her little finger.

"There," she said aloud to herself, "that will have to do."

She'd left the girls downstairs absorbed in their favourite game of the moment: "Warner Brothers". The rules were unfathomable and extremely fluid, very much dependent on Sarah's mood at the time. Today she was being particularly contrary with her sister, Joyce asking the whys and wherefores and Sarah arguing back so that Mabel, distracted by the constant bickering, abandoned her preparations in the bedroom to run back downstairs. "For goodness' sake, you kids! Can't you just stop arguing for two minutes!"

"Mummy, tell Joyce to stop whinging!" Sarah shouted back, unchastened. "Rules are rules and she keeps cheating!"

Mabel sighed. Picking up her best handbag from the hall stand, she took a last look in the mirror. The bodice was strained across her bust, but perhaps it was all the more stylish for that. "I'm going over the road," she called over her shoulder, opening the front door. "Just try and behave yourselves till I get back! I shan't be long." She slammed the door behind her in the hope the girls might be shocked into some kind of obedience.

Kay Hardy's garden was not as pretty as her own, Mabel was heartened to see. Bindweed straddled an unswept path and there were no nodding heads of Canterbury Bells to welcome any visitor that might call or cheerful marigolds to stud a freshly weeded flowerbed, as there were in her own. Indeed, the front garden seemed quite neglected, a rusty toy scooter flung upon the patchy grass near the gate, a pair of muddy football boots left to dry to a crust on the front step, an abandoned dolly, naked and legs akimbo, in a pram with a pink hood, no blankets and a wheel missing.

Mabel rang the doorbell; it chimed and Kay Hardy answered straight away, as though she had seen Mabel coming up the path. Her neighbour was dressed in a floral blouse with puffed sleeves and a pair of tailored khaki slacks, similar to the ones worn by the girls at the munitions factory during the war. Flat black pumps. A wide belt was most definitely made of real leather.

"Come in! Come in!" she said, smiling warmly. "I'll put the kettle on! Let's go through and sit in the garden. Best we enjoy the weather now it's stopped raining at last!"

Mabel followed Kay through the dimly lit passage, a naked 40-watt bulb its only illumination, her shoes tap-tapping on the Lino floor – no carpet. But any frugality here was immediately forgiven, because the kitchen was one of pure refinement as far as Mabel was concerned.

"Such a shame the young Queen had such a dreary day for her Coronation, and now see!"

Though she tried not to look to the left and right on her way through to the garden, Mabel could not help but envy the array of wall cupboards and worktops, the electric refrigerator and Formica-topped table with four matching chairs. A fruit bowl was brim full of bananas and tangerines. A glossy black cat, sitting tall and proud upon the windowsill, turned her head to stare, unblinking, as the visitor passed.

The black patent handbag felt strangely like one of Mr Jackson's stage props now, and Mabel held it to herself as she stepped through the back door onto a flag-stoned patio where two folding chairs were set around a wrought-iron table.

"Sit yourself down," invited Kay. "Oh goodness! I've forgotten the cushions for the chairs. I'll bring the tea in a jiffy. Do you take sugar?"

Mabel shook her head, though she did. "No, thank you." It wasn't polite to use up the sugar rations of others. Her handbag she tucked out of sight under the chair, smoothing the skirt of her best dress as she sat. She crossed her legs so the run in the stocking would be hidden.

"Now you just sit and take the weight off your feet," said Kay comfortably. "This is lovely. I was so afraid your family would keep you too busy to pop over! I've knocked on your door a couple of times but never found you in."

"Oh!" Mabel replied, "I must have been in the garden."

She had a precious few moments to compose herself as Kay went in to fetch the tea. The Hardys' garden was a thriving mass of weeds amongst scrubby grass, though an ancient cherry tree brought a sense of maturity her own did not have. Its only feature was a forlorn wooden shed which tilted slightly to one side, held steady by the happy circumstance that it leaned upon the back fence. A Jolly Roger flag, much frayed by weathering, hung from the gaping board above the door, secured there by a length of bedraggled Christmas ribbon.

Her hostess appeared back with a tray of cups and saucers, all mismatched, and a plate of biscuits. "It's still chilly for June," she said. "Are you going to be warm enough out here?" She placed the tray on the table and took up a spoon to stir the tea leaves in the pot.

"Oh, yes! I'm quite alright, thank you. How lush and green your grass is." Mabel said, for want of something more complimentary. "It must be all the rain we've had!"

"Don't you dare look at the flowerbeds," Kay's tone was light, her manner easy. "Bill has no interest in gardening, not like your Frank." She poured two cups and handed Mabel hers. "And I certainly don't want the job!" She offered the plate of biscuits to Mabel, who took one.

"Thank you. Yes, Frank's worked really hard on the garden," she said, glad she could describe something to be proud of. "It's been so lovely to move into such a friendly road." Mabel nibbled the chocolate biscuit, scooping a crumb from the corner of her mouth.

"Oh my dear," replied Kay with feeling, eyes wide, "you can't trust all the neighbours to be friendly!"

Mabel felt at a disadvantage now, unsure of how to reply. Who, exactly, did Kay Hardy think was not to be trusted?

There were a few moments of silence, Kay bending to stroke the cat who came to brush against her legs, tail held high. She did not elaborate on the nature of their neighbours, instead she continued, "What line of work is your Frank in?"

Mabel hesitated a little as she decided on a reply, for in truth Frank did a little of this and a little of that, as the mood took him. "He's very involved in his brother's greengrocery business," she said at last, taking a sip of her tea and keeping her voice level. "They've worked together for years. He can pretty much turn his hand to anything."

Kay smiled, showing no sign of anything Mabel might discern as suspicion. "My Bill has always worked at the abattoir. So useful during the rationing. We never go short of anything."

Conversation turned to the children, Kay's eldest being keen on netball, her middle daughter beginning to show real prowess in English, and her youngest his father's boy and apparently a promising footballer.

Mabel privately thought they should teach him to clean his boots; protect them with some Dubbin rather than leave them strewn about the path, out in all weathers.

"Exercise is so good for children," she said.

"What about your girls, Mabel? Are they settled at school? Do they have friends who come to tea? Little girls love that, don't they."

Mabel side-stepped the question. She told of Sarah's enjoyment of reading and Joyce's love of numbers. She explained to Kay that her parents were recently moved to Bristol from Blagdon, her father an engineer. She blushed a little at the exaggeration but continued.

Her sister Frances was married to an airman who had a position at Bristol Aircraft Works and they lived in their own bungalow near Weston-Super-Mare.

She did not mention the complication that was Clive. Time enough to do that when it became more necessary.

They spoke of the price of coal and a new recipe Mabel had found in *Woman's Weekly* for trifle sweetened with honey, and Kay reminded her that sugar and margarine rations were to be increased by the government, now the Coronation was done.

"Bill can always get you a pound of offal on the cheap, lites and liver and the like, and I know a good recipe for kidney pudding."

Mabel shuddered. "Oh, my goodness!" Quite horrified by the thought, she forgot not to be rude, "I'll never get my children to eat that!"

There was an awkward silence until Kay offered to make more tea, picking up the tray to go inside. The cat followed.

Mabel turned her attention to the garden to settle her nerves a little. The clouds parted and a welcome ray of sunshine glanced upon the roof of the shed where an amorous pigeon, puffed up to show his iridescent magnificence, was cooing and dipping before a prospective girlfriend.

"Don't we always appreciate an hour without the children," Kay said wistfully as she came back with the tray, and much to Mabel's relief not a bit less friendly than before. "Mine always go to their grandparents' on a Monday after school."

And Mabel came to her senses and remembered the girls, trusted to keep themselves busy and possibly, even now, up to mischief.

"I must go!" she said, quickly getting to her feet. "I'm so sorry to rush off but I mustn't stay for more tea." She bent to collect her bag. "But it's been lovely – to get to know you."

Kay showed her to the door, still smiling, insisting Mabel come again and they would have "a good natter". She opened the front door. "Perhaps I can come across to you next time?"

"Oh," Mabel said, flustered at the very thought, "I would ask you over, of course, but Frank is often catching up on his sleep . . . you know, after a night shift."

Her neighbour smiled, leaning against the door jamb as Mabel stepped through to the path. "Don't you worry yourself," she assured her. "You're welcome here anytime."

Mabel crossed the road, her steps light, smiling to herself. She felt it had gone well, this first visit. She recalled the warmth of the sun as she had sat, perfectly confident, exchanging pleasantries and simply chatting about this and that. It seemed to Mabel, now she had become someone who was invited out to tea, that even a common pigeon can look beautiful when sunlight dances upon its wings.

Walking up her own front path, Mabel bent to straighten the empty milk bottles upon the step and saw with quiet horror that two of the buttons on her bodice had popped open with the strain of sitting still in a neighbour's garden. And there, for all the world to see and as bold as brass, was her yellowed corset.

10

Bristol, 1954

The baby arrived during a stormy night in mid-February, Frank concerned and attentive, bringing Mabel a cup of tea once he heard the cry of a baby safely born. If he were disappointed it was not a boy, he didn't say. He borrowed an extra pillow from the children's bedroom and brought the layette that Mabel had knitted and left ready in the airing cupboard.

The children woke early, excited by the fuss and bother in their parents' room, thrilled to see the bundle that was their new baby sister.

"Up you come, girls!" Mabel said, using a free hand to help Joyce onto the bed though the violent movement of the springs caused her to wince in pain. "Look at what's happened in the night!"

And she tucked the shawl a little away from the baby's face so they might see the pink rosiness of her, and share in the wonder. "What shall we call her, girls?"

Unbeknownst to her Frank was already on his way to the Registry Office, where he was to write the baby's name as not Myra, as he and Mabel had decided, but Catherine, after a woman on Mrs Newson's television he particularly admired.

Mabel had used her Family Allowance to buy crayons and magazines she'd hoped to have five minutes to read before lending them to Kay, and the little girls sat upon her bed all morning long, drawing beautiful jewellery upon the ladies and curly black moustaches on the faces of the men. And each took their turn in cuddling their new baby, a little one welcomed into the world with an overflow of sisterly love, which smothered and blessed in equal measure.

11

Bristol, 1955

"Oh, Mabel, surely not!" Kay cried. "Another baby, and little Cath won't be much past her first birthday! How are you going to manage?"

They were sitting together in Kay's garden, a tray of tea before them on the wrought-iron table. It was early January and though the sky was a china blue, both women were wrapped up well in winter coats and headscarves worn in the manner of the young queen.

"How will you manage, Mabel?" she repeated, her face a picture of concern. "Five children! You'll have your work cut out."

"Clive's not home very often so it's four, really," answered Mabel, as much to herself as to Kay, the conversation one she had been dreading.

"Well," her friend topped up their cups and set the teapot down on the tray with more gusto than was needed, "you'd best get yourself to the clinic once this baby's arrived. Times have changed and there's a lot to be done now, to stop them coming."

Mabel didn't stay long; she had done what she had set out to do and broken the news. Frank would be wanting his tea.

When she walked back into the kitchen, just an hour to spare before collecting children from school, Frank was seated at a kitchen table scattered in brown envelopes and scraps of paper with long, neat columns of calculations. He looked up as she came in, and for a moment she saw a flicker of uncertainty in his eyes.

"Hello, Frank, you're home early." Mabel kept her voice light.

"George has cut my hours," he replied. "He's taken on a young lad to do the running around. Says it's cheaper."

Mabel ran the tap, took up her apron and sprinkled soap powder into the washing-up water. She swished it round to melt the flakes.

"That doesn't seem fair, when you've always put yourself out for him," she said. "Where does that leave us? With the bills, I mean."

Frank collected up the envelopes and papers, tucking them into an inside pocket and sliding the pencil behind his ear. "I've found us a business proposition. A bakery along Ashley Road. It could be a nice little earner, one way and another."

Mabel could not decide on a reply. She slid plates and saucers into the washing-up bowl.

"I'm going across there tomorrow. I can wait for you to get back from taking the kids to school if you're interested in coming. It will need the two of us to get it started – there's no money for taking anyone on."

Mabel propped the dishes on the draining board to dry, speckles of soap powder lingering on the china, and took off her apron.

"I'm going to school," she said. "We can talk later. I didn't think you knew the first thing about baking!"

It was a dreary place, a pre-war, square concrete block with green double doors to the street and a single frosted window set high up in the wall, all badly in need of a fresh coat of paint.

"Come on," Frank parked the van at the kerb, "I've got the keys. The bloke said to just let ourselves in."

"Where's the shop?" He didn't answer. She took Cath in her arms and climbed gingerly from the van, supporting the weight of her stomach with her free hand. She followed him in, double doors creaking open on rusty hinges, musty air and gloom reminding her of the caves she and Jane had explored as children, up in the Combe.

"Leave the door open, Mabe," suggested Frank, "let some air in the place."

Mabel had no experience of bakeries, but even she could see the shoddiness of the fittings and the filthy grease of many years around the edges of the ancient oven door. She put Cath down, a wriggling toddler too much to manage.

Frank opened the door of the oven to inspect the workings. "Needs a bit of cleaning up with a wire brush."

"This doesn't seem the right thing to go for, Frank." Even in the half light, Mabel could see the limitations. "Best you come up with a different idea."

"Can't do that, Mabe," he answered, bending to peer into the depths of the oven. "I've already paid the bloke a month's rent."

"I don't think I can do it, Kay - work in that bakery, I mean." Mabel stared into the distance as the women sat in the quietness of the Hardys' garden the following morning, a day when winter sun slanted through skeletal trees though there was no warmth in it. "I can turn my hand to anything in the kitchen – but this! Baking bread and cakes in industrial amounts for factories! And me with a baby due in a few months! And you know the troubles I've had before . . ." She put her teacup back on its saucer. "No, I don't think I can do it."

Mabel looked out across Kay's garden, still a mass of scrubby grass and dandelions but comfortably familiar to her now, after so many easy visits and cups of tea in whatever the weather. Because confidences could be shared more easily, more safely in a garden across the road.

The shed had recently breathed its last, now just a pile of rough wood in the corner of the garden. No amorous pigeon, sun dancing on lilac wings, would be roosting there come the spring; a mouse might take shelter, perhaps, or more likely a rat. Mabel knew about rats in sheds.

"What do you think I should do? Frank says there's no money, and what we did have has gone on the rent for that bakery!"

"Looks like you don't have much choice, Mabe." Kay reached out a hand to touch Mabel gently on her knee. "Do it afraid," she said, quietly. "You'll have to do it afraid. Then get up the next day and do it again."

And Mabel, not daring to meet her friend's eyes, remembered the bulk and strength of Kay's husband, his loud voice and overbearing manner, and wondered.

They christened him John, a bright and bonny child with tight golden curls and a lusty cry which woke the house at all hours and caused Frank to curse the nuisance of him. The only blessing was the glorious June weather so Mabel could push the pram into the garden, Cath playing dollies under the kittiwake blue of a midsummer sky while Mabel cleared the chaos of the day before, and scrambled dinner from next to nothing so there would be something on the table when Frank came in.

Three weeks in and he expected her back at work. "I can't keep on, Mabe," he told her, exhausted after a sixteen-hour day and looking forward to a scant four hours in bed before getting up to do it all over again. "It's a two-man job, I told you. You're not pulling your weight."

She took a wooden spoon to stir the nappies, coming up to the boil in an enamel bucket on the cooker. "It's just not possible, Frank," she said. "You're fooling yourself. It was always going to be impossible. I've been talking to my friend Kay and she said—"

She hadn't heard him get up from the table and cross the floor, had no time to dodge the hand that came across her face, had no thought of crying out because never in her life before had she known the back of a man's hand.

Mabel turned again to the pan, stirring the nappies so they churned and writhed one upon another in an angry, rolling boil.

12

Bristol, 1956

The house, which had once promised them a new beginning, demanded rent money, water rates and the reliability of a regular pay packet. The brown envelopes behind the clock were left unopened, the coal man got no answer at the door though he knocked long and hard with a good deal of shouting, and George was owed money from winnings at the dog track that Frank had pocketed and reinvested on a sure thing. The benefit of their own front door was lost in the inconvenient responsibility of its upkeep.

Frank's working hours with his brother had dwindled to little more than two half days; he took up a rag and bone round with the van, coming home after tea to tip the sacks of miscellany upon the kitchen floor for Mabel to sort, though first she must step over and amongst it to finish getting the children ready for bed.

"See if there's anything there that will do the kids," he suggested, smiling at Mabel, pleased with himself, Mabel supposed, for providing for his family.

She smelled the detritus of a hundred unknown lives; to dress her children in the cast-offs of others – this is what it had come to. She vowed never to wear anything from the heaps herself. Tearing to shreds the women's dresses she found there, she made multicoloured rag rugs for each of the bedroom doorways.

Mabel heard the rattle of the letterbox and the whistling of the postman as he made his way next door to Mrs Newson's. She stopped in her tidying of the kitchen to check the doormat and there it was, a letter from Jane. Time enough, then, to sort the kitchen later. She wiped her hands on her apron and put the kettle on, making tea while the letter lay, unopened, on the kitchen table. It was not right to rush the reading of it.

Mabel's reply, the envelope waiting for a moment when she could find a stamp, was still on the kitchen table when Frank came in from work. He demanded to know what she'd written about; what she'd told her sister about Frank's work. What Jane had been told about the falling-out with George.

"Nothing," assured Mabel, bringing his tea to the table on her way upstairs to check on the babies. "We tell each other about the children – the usual things, really, Laura and Father, I've asked about work, what's going on in West Harptree, you know—"

"I'm out tonight," he interrupted, picking up his knife and fork to eat. "I'll be back late. I've promised to meet someone down the track. At nine."

She busied herself at the sink. Goodness only knew where the money for the dog racing was going to come from. She wiped her hands and called the girls in from the garden.

"Get yourselves ready for bed, you two," Mabel told them, "and don't wake the little ones when you go up."

Frank rose from the table, dinner half finished, and reached for his coat. "Sarah is coming with me," he said.

Mabel couldn't answer for a moment; this was a new game and she wasn't sure how to play. "It's a school day tomorrow, Frank," she said quietly. "She can't stay out late."

"Get your hairbrush and something to tidy yourself up with," Frank told his daughter.

When Sarah had done as she was asked, wordless, Frank caught her to him and dragged the brush through her hair, all of a tangle since the game in the garden. "Stand still!" he demanded, the child brought to tears.

Mabel had no weapon against this.

"Frank," she implored, "be careful! What on earth do you think you're doing?"

He took Sarah by the wrist and picked up his van keys, and Mabel saw the anger in him and stepped forwards. "Frank, this is senseless . . ." she began, though she could see he was in no mood to listen, and as he wrenched the child towards the door she saw the flat of his hand come towards her. Taken by surprise, she fell to the floor, cracking her shoulder against the wall so she cried out.

Frank stepped over her, dragging the child by the wrist.

She heard the van door slam, the engine roar into life, the belch of the exhaust as Frank pulled away.

Joyce reached out a hand to her mother, as though a six-year-old child could lift a grown woman off the floor.

"Up you go to bed, Joyce," she kept her voice level, struggling onto her knees though her head was spinning. "Sarah will be back soon. Take your torch so you can read in bed. A special treat."

She took the tea towel and ran cold water from the tap, holding the cloth to her face to take the worst of the sting from her cheek. She needed to sit for a little while. To think. She leaned her elbows on the table, water from the teacloth trickling down inside the sleeves of her cardigan. For a fleeting moment she considered crossing the road to knock on Kay's door, but the thought of Bill answering it chased the idea from her mind.

Staring into nothingness, her eyes fell upon the mantelpiece where the collection of brown envelopes were crammed into the space between clock and wall. She put the cloth down upon the table and heaved herself to her feet, wiping wet hands on the skirts of her dress. She took the bundle of letters, sitting once again to shuffle through the pile until she came to one bearing the postmark "Bristol City Council Housing Department". She replaced the others behind the clock.

Filling the kettle, she waited patiently for it to boil before holding the letter to the spout, taking care to keep her fingers from the steam. The flap of the envelope lifted.

Seven days, then, to get out. Mabel checked the date on the letter again, just to be sure. Seven days from last Wednesday. Tomorrow, then.

She took herself to bed, though she didn't undress. A hot water bottle brought some relief to her shoulder. Well after dark she heard Frank and Sarah come in, footsteps on the stairs, the quiet closing of the girls' bedroom door. He later climbed into bed beside her but she did not move or speak. Her back was to him. The letter, in a moment of brazen defiance, she had left open on the kitchen table.

"We can only shift a vanful," Frank told her as she stirred porridge, anxious the girls would not be late for school on what was to be their last day. "Let's go as soon as the kids get home."

"Where? Where shall we go?" She filled bowls, sprinkled sugar, sorted the babies' bottles, found and folded a clean nappy and lifted John into his pram to change him so he could not squirm and roll away while she did.

"I've found a job with a house," he told her. "It's a waste of time, keep giving rent money to the council. No future in that; it's a fool's game."

Mabel believed all eyes might be on her as she took the girls to school, though the public shaming of bailiffs at the door was yet to begin.

"Hurry home tonight," she told the girls as they parted at the school gate. "You're old enough to walk home together, just be careful as you cross the road."

"I've been asking you for ages if we could!" Joyce was triumphant.

"We're going out with Daddy," Mabel continued, "so hurry home, as I say. No dawdling." She turned the pram homeward and walked quickly away so that Joyce could not ask a thousand questions, grateful she did not meet Kay because the chiffon scarf she had twisted about her neck did not completely cover the red flush on her cheek.

"Bye, Mummy," Sarah called after her mother. "We can run all the way home! Don't worry, I promise we won't be late!"

There was a note on the doormat when she turned the key in the latch. "Mabe, I've knocked a couple of times, but no answer. How are things? Fancy a cup of tea later? Anytime to suit you. I'm in all day."

She packed school uniforms all in one bag, space enough at the top to take her two favourite cookery books and a copy of *Sorrell and Son*, given to her by Kay for Christmas and not yet read. The other books she threw on the bonfire Frank had going in the back garden. Flames licked at the pear tree so she feared for its safety. Sparks flew.

Tea towels and aprons all went into a crate; sugar, tea and porridge into a cardboard box she found in the understairs cupboard. Her hands shook with the hurry of it.

Her bruised shoulder aching with the bending and carrying she took a moment to walk from room to room, looking here and there for things that mattered – though nothing, really, mattered enough to care. Caring meant feeling, and she must not allow herself that.

It was important there was room enough for the pram. She wouldn't leave that behind. Wheeling it out to the kerb she saw he was juggling one box with another, doing his very best to fill every corner of the van. She left him to it, walking back into the house and needing to step aside so two burly strangers could pass, carrying her glass table – the one given to her by Kay when she and Bill redecorated their bedroom. She wondered what they had done with her bottle of Midnight in Paris eau de cologne, bought for her by Frank after a success in the St Leger.

Mabel emptied the last of the food from the larder, throwing the crust of the loaf out for the birds and emptying the teapot into a flowerbed. She sprinkled Vim into the sink and scrubbed it clean with a scourer, running the tap until the porcelain shone and sparkled in the afternoon sunlight. Through the kitchen window, she saw her little family of sparrows flutter down to the feast. A dunnock appeared from beneath the hedge to fight for its share.

Mabel heard the children come in from school, calling for her in voices that held a note of fear.

"Mummy!" called Sarah. "Mrs Hardy met me at the gate and said she's been knocking at the door but you didn't answer and is there anything she can do?"

She took off her flowery apron, draping it across the sink just as though she would simply be picking it up later, and tying it around her waist to get tea. Because, in truth, she was leaving something of herself here, in this place of loveliness.

13

―――――⊚⊙⊚―――――

Farmborough, 1956

The village of Farmborough lay just fifteen miles to the south of Bristol, so there was plenty of daylight left when Frank pulled up at a row of terraced cottages barely an hour after leaving Lockleaze. The three older children were crammed into the gap between boxes and front seats, the baby snuggled on Sarah's lap, asleep. Once Frank switched off the engine John woke up with a howl of protest, limbs thrashing, struggling to be free.

Mabel felt the judder of the van, the excited restlessness of children at her shoulder, the eagerness of Frank as he wound up the window and took his cigarettes and matches from the dashboard in readiness to begin again.

"Can you have a look for John's bottle of milk, Frank? Now he's awake he'll be hungry, he's had no tea," were the first words she had spoken since climbing into the van.

Frank jumped down to the road. "Yep – give me two minutes," he said obligingly, "Come on, you kids." Sliding open the side door, he stood back to let the children tumble out. "The keys are under the doormat."

"I'll go!" Sarah held the protesting baby out to her mother, "I'm the oldest!"

Mabel, cradling John against her shoulder, slammed the door shut with her free hand and turned to see where Frank had brought them.

"Hodgekins Row" declared a rusty plaque high up on the masonry. Six brick-built cottages with slate roofs and a row of chimney pots, and all grey, so very grey. Mabel could see no sign of life in gardens to either side, though a curtain twitched in an upstairs window next door. Further along the lane, farm buildings sprawled towards the road in a tangled arrangement of corrugated iron and slatted boards, barn doors swinging open. A derelict tractor leant against the fence at a crazy angle, one wheel missing, left to rust there in its own time. A tethered nanny goat ceased browsing to turn her head, watching Mabel with idle curiosity.

Beyond the terrace were fields and hedges as far as the eye could see, a batch in the near distance piled high with discarded waste from the coal mines. Mabel was back in her home county, but it wasn't a Somerset she recognised.

"Come on in!" Frank called cheerily from the front door. "Wait 'til the kids see the garden!" He came to lift the pram from the back of the van, as jaunty as she'd ever known him to be.

She placed the pram pillow to rights, took the baby's dummy from her pocket and offered it, strapped him in and wheeled the pram down the path. The front room was a gloomy affair, daylight filtered through a grimy pane, the air stale and not breathed in for many months. They passed through a low doorway, even Frank having to duck his head, into a kitchen of sorts beyond.

She shivered, a summer dress no match for the chill of this back scullery. She wheeled the pram to where John could see through the window and be amused for a while. "Let's get the van unloaded, then, while it's still daylight." Her tone was light, provoking his anger too dangerous. "It looks like they've taken all the electric lightbulbs out."

Frank made off back to the road and she looked about her. A stone sink was chipped and stained from a century of use with a tap suspended from above on a length of lead pipe, a grey rag twisted about its neck. At the window a yellowed net curtain was strung from a length of cane, propped at each end on cup hooks. On the far wall of the scullery a solid fuel range, empty of life, squatted beneath a red-brick fireplace speckled with ash. Blackened by soot and the lid half cocked, a cast-iron kettle stood upon an ancient gas stove.

"Here," Frank was bending to rummage in the box he'd set on the floor, finding a packet of rusks. "This will keep young John quiet for a few minutes while we get sorted." He thrust a biscuit into the child's eager hand and Mabel felt the betrayal of a baby so easily placated by a father showing a rare moment of concern.

Sarah appeared beside her, face animated; she took her mother's hand as though to pull her into the garden. "Mummy, there are fields and woods and everything!" Flushed with the prospect of adventure, she was eager to be gone. "I've seen them from upstairs. And Joyce is already climbing over the wall at the end of the garden . . . see? She'll go without us if we don't hurry!"

Mabel couldn't think quite how long she had stood, looking at nothing in particular.

"Why are you crying?" The girl looked up into Mabel's face. "Don't you like the country? Look – there are cows peeping over the back wall! Aren't you coming to explore with us?"

Mabel wiped her wet cheeks with her sleeve. She saw the concern and felt the tightening of the hand in her own. "I'll come another time. I've got things to sort here. You go off and have fun with Joyce." She pushed her daughter towards the door. "Don't go too near the cows now – they kick if the fancy takes them. And be back soon for some tea!"

"It's so *lovely* here, Mummy!" chirruped Sarah as she scampered into the garden, imploring her sister to "Wait for me!"

Frank carried boxes in from the van, dumping them randomly on the stone floor of the scullery. "Fill that kettle and make us a cup of tea, Mabe," he said to her back. "Where's the box we emptied the larder into?" He didn't wait for an answer. "I've only just turned the water on, so let it run for a bit. I'll soon be finished with the van."

"Frank, I want to go back." Her voice scarcely more than a whisper, she sensed he was still there, straightening up, watching her.

"We can't. Don't be daft."

His tone was softer; hope grew. "This is awful. We can't stay here." She turned from the window so Frank might see her grief. She remembered Blagdon – when they'd met together on The Mead in the dead of night. "It'll be alright," he'd said. "We can get our own place . . ."

Frank, meeting her eyes for little more than a heartbeat, bent again to his task. He found the box of food he was searching for. "Here we are, here's the stuff we packed up from the kitchen. There's milk on the doorstep. Buck up, we'll soon have this place ship-shape."

She ran the water as she'd been told, filled the kettle from the tap, handed the baby another rusk and collected the milk from the step without raising her eyes to see if the neighbours were still watching. And all the while, Frank was unloading metal bed frames and boxes of blankets and clothes they had so hastily thrown together just a few hours before, taking only what the bailiffs saw no value in.

14

Farmborough, 2020

I collect Sarah from Bristol mid-morning and we drive the fifteen miles to Farmborough. I can see she is looking forward to the day; she talks about the memories she has of that cottage in the country, the games she and Joyce played together in the fields beyond the garden wall, the cows they came to know by name.

"Oh, my word!" Sarah sits back in her seat as I park the car. "She hated it here! I can still see her standing in that awful scullery, crying, while he took all their stuff out the van and dumped it on the floor all around her! We should have realised how miserable she was, and helped more."

Eleven-year-olds cannot make it right, I want to say, no matter how hard they try. And I wonder – how is it that a young child is given her mother's unhappiness to carry?

We walk from a cul-de-sac of crowded newbuilds down the slope to the main road, towards the cottage where we spent a year or two of our childhoods. Sarah is lagging slightly behind me.

I am concerned her thoughts are elsewhere. "Let's be careful how we cross." We have never, ever in our lives held hands, so we certainly don't now. In our later years we might perhaps learn to walk arm in arm, discovering the pleasure of a physical closeness we never saw modelled, but for now we keep our distance.

The traffic is constant, roaring past us so that having dashed across to the middle, we are standing in a wind tunnel hedged about by trucks and cars belching smoke as they change gear to take the hill.

Hodgekins Row is an insignificant row of unremarkable square boxes, set side by side in pairs, each a mirror image of its neighbour. Front gardens are stony with tufts of yellowed grass struggling here and there to proliferate into something more respectable. There are no flowers. I see Sarah is disappointed, because she has misremembered and this row of shabby dwellings could never be mistaken for pretty country cottages.

"Which one was ours?" I ask my big sister as we stand on the scrubby verge next to an open gateway.

"This one, number three. Our father used to prop the gate closed with an old brick." She is not looking at me but is lost somewhere in the years between then and now. "He never did mend the hinge for her."

"Was that the path to the back garden?" I point to the scruffy walkway between numbers two and three. "Is that where we kept the chickens? Before the fire in the Anderson?"

We go as close as we dare, peering into the gloom of a covered side passage littered with dustbins and a pile of old newspapers caught up with string; a crate of empty beer bottles. The houses on each side seem deserted so I'm hoping there's no real danger of being accosted.

"The garden looks so small," says Sarah in wonder, "but it always seemed enormous to us! It's like it happened only yesterday." Speaking as though to herself, she walks two paces behind me as we make our way back to the car, dodging the traffic on the A39 to cross the road. "I think this must have been the place where she gave up any last hope of having a nice home."

It's too profound to warrant a flippant reply. And anything more elaborate would be a fabrication on my part because I have no recollection of my mother here at all. I can't picture her, or remember her wearing a favourite dress, or hear her voice in my head saying my name. Even as I stand within a few metres of where she cooked and cleaned and hung washing upon a line, or stepped from the front door to push the pram to the village shop, I can't recall her eyes crinkling in a smile, or the feeling of being held tightly to her – for surely she would have, from time to time, scooped me up? Hugged me to herself? Perhaps, I think, her love for my little brother might have superseded any thought of my preciousness, the baby girl for whom she once saved sixpences in a jar.

15

Bristol, 1956

Lincoln Street was a road of two-up-two-down houses set in the maze of back streets just a mile or so from Bristol city centre. The red-brick terraces on either side were blackened by a century and a half of smoke and smut from industrial chimneys still visible above the rooftops, though the factories were long gone. The front door of each house opened directly onto the street, and every corner boasted either a shop, an off-licence or a public house.

After the wilderness of Farmborough Mabel felt the variety of it. It was a neighbourhood where mothers could push prams to the shops on the very next corner and little girls might play hopscotch on a pavement marked up with chalk.

As she watched, a front door opened and a child, in kilt and scarlet jumper, ran to join a gathering of friends with skipping ropes across the street; a woman appeared round the corner with a babe in arms, calling "Mornin'!" to an acquaintance across the road, who in turn raised a hand in greeting and walked on. An older man in a raincoat and cloth cap walked briskly in the direction of the off-licence, pipe held to his mouth and a newspaper tucked under his arm, for all the world as though he had somewhere important to be; a woman in a hairnet and overall with a besom broom in her hand swept the pavement outside the pub in readiness for opening time. It was community. Mabel held her baby closer, and saw the possibility of it.

"Ooh look!" piped up Sarah to her mother, "eighteen and twenty! It's got two numbers!"

Mabel marvelled at her children's ability to keep believing their father would forever bring them bigger and better things.

Frank unlocked the door of the shop and stepped aside as the children, Mabel following, pushed past. She found the light switch and flicked it on. In an instant the shop was bright and cheerful, freshly painted a pale primrose yellow, glass shelves across the full length of one wall and extending the width of the window.

"Look at this, Mabe!" Frank said, wonder in his voice. "Not bad, eh?" He smiled round at them all. "Nice big window, plenty of shelves and the street already looks busy. We should do well here, Mabe, plenty of space for us to show what we're made of!"

Mabel sensed his excitement, saw his ambition, understood the delusion.

"It's a wonderful shop, Frank," she reassured her husband, "and just as you said, an opportunity to make good through our own endeavours. They never appreciated you in Farmborough."

"Let's have a look round the back." He led the way through to a living room, directly off the back of the shop. It wasn't large, certainly for a family of seven. There was no floor covering. The fireplace was a tiled affair, empty save for a few bits of scrunched up newspaper singed brown at the edges and sprinkled in freshly fallen soot; Mabel sensed the acrid burn of it in her nostrils. A side window looked out onto the blank wall of a covered alleyway.

"That goes through to the bake house. Nice and convenient for you, Mabe!"

The scullery had barely space enough for a table and chairs. A stone sink leant against the far wall – not unlike Farmborough, but perhaps cleaner. A boiler for the hot water stood in the corner, a coal scuttle beside it half full; under the window overlooking the backyard a cast-iron gas stove stood on tall legs beside a kitchen cabinet, painted green.

She could make a difference here once she'd set her mind to it; given time, much could be done to make it homely.

"I shall miss the cows, Mummy," said Joyce, following half a step behind Mabel. "Are there any fields to explore, do you think? Can me and Sarah go and see?"

"Come on," their father's voice was loud and confident, "I'll show you the bakehouse."

Of course, Mabel realised, this was where Frank had cleared off to the previous week when he'd not gone into work. She felt the deceit of it. And he paid a deposit on the rent, he told her, so that solved the mystery of the Family Allowance missing from her purse.

With an air of proprietorship Frank now showed her the wooden work benches, surfaces scoured clean and pitted, bowed by fifty years of kneading and cutting. He unlatched the door to the store room and pointed out the well-stocked shelves and the sacks of flour. Mouse droppings speckled the dirt floor.

"There's plenty of room beneath these workbenches to store the fruit and sugars," he told her, and with a special pride and not a little excitement he showed the children the huge dough machine, the bowl the size of a water butt. Attachments of every description were hung neatly to one side of the mixer, and taking up the entire width of one wall, two coke-fired ovens were built into the brick, stacked one upon the other.

"These are the jewels in the crown!" Frank told her, Mabel wondering where on earth the expression had come from. "And all fired up and ready to go!"

Wooden peels, six feet long and scorched black by years of use, stood to attention at each side.

"This is the stuff of dreams for a baker! Better than anything my old boss had at Farmborough! Look, Mabe." He unlatched both oven doors so they swung open and the children leapt back from the blast of heat that came at them from the furnace within. "The landlord promised he'd fire them up for me so we can make a start straightaway, see." He slammed the doors closed, latching them tight shut, his face flushed with excitement and warmth from the flames combined.

"It's a wonderful bakehouse, Frank," she replied. She lifted John more securely onto her hip, reaching to grab Cath's hand as the toddler made to explore beneath the flour troughs. "I'll go and make a start on the unpacking."

She wouldn't let herself think about the running of the shop, not yet, for really she had not one idea about the doing of it. And after so many months of exile in Farmborough, she truly could not remember how to start a conversation, let alone make polite small talk with customers.

Frank had found a new enthusiasm for life, up with the lark and eager to begin as his own boss once again. She enjoyed the relief of him leaving her alone, her husband working late into the night, even dinner eaten in the bakehouse so he could continue the task of kitting it out with more shelving, filling troughs with flour, sugar, dried fruits and oats, stacking tins and trays just as he preferred and cleaning every last trace of vermin from the storeroom.

Frank ordered coke for the ovens and sorted an account with the wholesalers so he could stock up on ingredients as and when he needed. He opened a bank account, he told Mabel with some pride, showing her his new chequebook, his name printed in ink at the bottom of each and every page. Now the world, he said, was his oyster. There was no stopping them.

The "Grand Opening" was, indeed, a grand success. Frank had done himself proud, though he'd had to work from dawn to dusk to get it finished.

Split tins crusty and warm from the oven, egg-washed cottage loaves, perfectly round and each one identical to the next, Eccles cakes bursting with fruit, and fat, fluffy jam doughnuts rolled in warm sugar. Apple turnovers, lardy cakes, currant buns and Genoese, vanilla slices and custard tarts dotted with nutmeg, bread pudding fragrant with spices and top and tailed with shortcrust pastry sprinkled in brown sugar. Fritters with just five currants apiece – counted out by children home from school and eager to help – warm and inviting and stacked in fragrant, lemony heaps upon the glass counter.

Once the shop door opened, the bell hardly stopped jangling; so busy was Mabel as one day followed another that she had no chance to sew or mend, or push the pram to the park for an outing, or take and fetch the older girls to and from school. They must fend for themselves in this world of Family Business. There weren't enough hours in the day to shop for vegetables or cook a proper dinner or iron perfect pleats into school gymslips.

Mabel put aside her plans for settling in. She sent Sarah to the corner shop for notepaper and envelopes, writing to Bristol Blind School with their new address though making it quite clear that Clive could not be accommodated at home until the October half term. She penned a quick note to Jane to tell her they had made the move back to Bristol and all was well. She wrote to Kay, telling her the good news.

"Call in for a cup of tea if you're passing," she wrote, "I'm always here!" After the loneliness of Farmborough it felt good to see the words on the page in black and white to prove to herself it was all true.

Mabel woke with a start, the dull light of early morning creeping through uncurtained windows. For a moment she lay very still, feeling the weight and warmth of her husband pressing against her back and the scratchiness of the army blanket against her face. Twelve months in and she still expected to see the blue of the wide Farmborough skies, to hear the rustle and scrape of the old apple tree against their bedroom window or the bawling of the cows, barging and complaining as they were hustled into the barn for milking.

"Frank! Time to wake up!" she whispered, fearful of waking John in the cot beside them, "It's time to get going!"

Mabel nudged him with an elbow, throwing the blanket back and stepping out onto the bare Lino. She stumbled over her shoes in the half light.

"Frank, that delivery to Wills mustn't be late again!" Shivering and still wearing her slip and underwear from the day before, she reached for her blouse and skirt from the chair by the bed.

Frank stirred. "Bring us a cup of tea, Mabe."

She dressed, running a comb through her hair though she had no mirror. Then tea for Frank, a piece of toast to keep her going, milk in the pan ready for Sarah to warm for the babies' bottles.

It was impossible, this contract with the tobacco factory. No matter how early they rose from their beds, how quickly he weighed, mixed, moulded and proved, never was that canteen order ready for a nine o'clock delivery.

Mabel left the kitchen in the usual half-finished chaos. The bakehouse was eternally warm – a blessing when the mornings were chilly and her fingers stiff and clumsy. She took up the brush to grease the tins, working ahead of Frank as he moulded the warm dough this way and that, a steady rhythm of hand and wrist, poetry in motion, loaves of every genre beautifully formed by the skill of his hands.

They fell easily to their tasks – she lining up the straps of bread tins, greasing them, Frank dropping in the dough – never needing to use the scales, each one near enough two pounds. Then the bread rolls for the Wills tobacco factory – moulded at speed, two by two and placed onto greased trays, left to prove in the warmer; Mabel brushing on the egg wash ready for the blast of the oven and the rolls reappearing, in good time, melded together as a hundred conjoined twins.

Not yet seven o'clock in the morning and Mabel had already been on her feet for two hours. "Frank, I need to get the kids up," she reminded him, knowing they were up against time, feeling his weariness with the lifting, the moulding, the bending, the stretching deep into the roar of the furnace to flip the tins with the wooden peel, shuffling one strap with another so the loaves might share the heat more evenly and be perfectly baked.

"Don't be long, then," he replied, not turning from the task, eyes squinting, face flushed crimson and sweat on his forehead. "There's the pikelets and doughnuts to finish off yet, and all to get over to Bedminster by nine o'clock."

She called down the alleyway, lifting her voice above the clatter of the dough machine,

"Girls, can you get the little ones up and sort their breakfast? You've got time before school."

"But Mummy," wailed Joyce, ever the complainer, "I've been late every day this week and it's class assembly this morning!"

It was of no matter. She couldn't find the patience to argue, not this morning. Frank had been particularly terse with her and the varicose veins in her legs were playing up. She put the egg wash down and went through to the kitchen. "Just help me out, will you! You've got a few minutes. And don't forget Mrs Dunn's loaf!"

"Oh Mummy, no! Not Mrs Dunn!" Sarah left the bread and jam on her plate to go in search of cardigan and school bag. "She takes ages to come to the door!"

Mabel sighed, finding dishes and spoons in yesterday's greasy washing-up water, fetching the milk from the back step. She reached for the box of cornflakes on the shelf above the table.

"Just be quick. Now, I've got to get back to Daddy – no more moaning. Shout through when you're going."

Half an hour later and Sarah was yelling. The little ones were crying – she heard Joyce raise her voice to them. In a house where children watched children, the dangers of open fires and cellar steps gave her no peace.

Mabel wiped her hands on a dishrag and turned her back on the bread tins for a moment to call through the alleyway, "What's the problem? You know we're busy out here!" It was impossible to hear the child over the ear-splitting thrum of the bread mixer. She put her head round the kitchen door.

"Mummy, I need a towel for swimming. It's today."

"Oh, for goodness' sake, Sarah! Couldn't you have asked me last night?"

"Mummy, you were too busy. Remember? All you did was tell me to be quiet!"

"There's one in the dirty washing basket. Take that. Mrs Dunn's loaf is just on the counter in the shop."

Mabel heard the door slam as they left, Sarah shouting at her sister to hurry. The little ones had been finding their own mischief in the kitchen and a puddle of milk sat upon the floor, a bowl of cereal upturned on the table with a lively game of "catch" going on, in and out the chair legs.

"Come on, you nippers," she stooped to gather John in her arms, holding out a hand to the toddler. "Let's go upstairs and get dressed. Then we can all watch Daddy in the bakery."

It was ten to nine. No time, then, for that cup of tea before she unlocked the shop door and turned the sign to "Open".

Little ones in the bakehouse with Frank, Mabel hunted through the ironing basket to find a clean pinny. She combed her hair, taking the little pot of rouge to smudge her cheeks, perfecting her lipstick before the mirror with the end of a little finger. Pursing her lips, she leant in to check the lipstick had not smudged.

Once through in the shop, she checked the till for small change and topped up the stock of white paper bags hanging from a string at the end of the counter. When Frank needed to leave on the delivery, she settled the little ones in the pram and wheeled it out to the pavement, strapping the baby in and sitting Cath at his feet. They did well enough there – passers-by always ready to stop and say hello, to smile and ask, "And how are you today?"

And very soon the bell jangled and the first customers of the day came in. Mabel forgot her weariness and her tired and aching legs, and smiled prettily, greeting each customer by name as though they were an old friend. She was especially proud of herself for this bravery. Who would have thought it? From the hostility of Farmborough to the neighbourly streets of Barton Hill, and she was holding her own.

She wrapped warm, crusty loaves in fine tissue paper, and slipped cream cakes and Battenberg slices into little white bags. She added up the total and handed out the change. She took an order for a three-tier wedding cake, carefully noting down the names of the happy couple, and assured Mrs Worth from Barrow Road the Russian Slices were fresh today – knowing full well that Frank fashioned them out of stale cake left over from the day before, mixed generously with warmed raspberry jam.

And when, during a lull in customers, a tall, bull-necked man in a black overcoat and bowler hat walked in, Mabel, smiling, fully expected him to ask for a farmhouse, or a split tin. Instead, and with a suddenness that shocked, he leaned across the counter, his face so uncomfortably close to Mabel's she could see his yellowed plastic teeth and smell his fetid kipper breath. He spat words at her so she felt the spray of his spittle on her cheek.

"Tell that husband of yours . . ." and here the terrible bulk of the man took a breath, "that I've been very patient while you get this business on its feet, but it's doing very well, as any fool can see, and he owes me four weeks' rent!"

He paused, whether for effect or in readiness to hurl abuse at her, Mabel could not tell. Time stood still. Her heart racing, she had the presence of mind to take a step back before the man straightened up and continued, eyes bulging in his round, unshaven face, "And I am *not* a patient man!"

He crossed the floor, turning to look at Mabel as he opened the door to leave, brass bell jangling into a frenzy above his head. "Tell him I'll be back Friday," he said. "Early."

The door slammed shut behind him.

Mabel sat down hard on the stool, her knees threatening to give way. She could taste the man's fishy breath in her mouth, feel the menace in his words, see the smudged sweat of his fat fingerprints upon the glass of the countertop.

After a minute or two she walked to the shop door, turning the cardboard sign to "closed" and throwing the catch. She went through to the kitchen to make herself a cup of tea. Her hands shook as she filled the kettle at the tap and struggled to fit the lid.

When Frank came back from Wills and asked why she'd closed the shop early Mabel told him about the landlord's visit, keeping her voice steady so he would not be angered.

He interrupted her story, waving his hand dismissively. "You don't want to worry about old Clack! His bark's worse than his bite." He poured himself a mug of tea from the pot. "I'll sort the rent," he said, taking his tea through to the bakery. "Two weeks' worth will keep him happy."

When Friday came, she knew of no plan that might prepare them for the landlord's visit. Indeed she'd had a terrible time getting Frank from his bed, the bread rolls for the Wills' order already an hour late going into the prover.

"Frank, Clack will be calling again today," she ventured, "He told me: Friday."

She continued to grease trays, setting them in a row on the work bench, lining up the straps of bread tins so he might more easily reach them. There was no way the order was going to be through on time. "He came again yesterday, to remind us. I told you," she persisted. "You were out. He wasn't nice."

He busied himself weighing flour and fat.

"Frank, where's the rent money gone? You said you were taking it down last week. I told you – Clack has called for his money more than once and you said you had it sorted."

"It's no odds, Mabel! Stop the nagging!" Frank threw the giant dough hook across the bench so it skittered away from her onto the floor, narrowly missing her feet. Taking up the cutter he sliced into the lump of fat with unnecessary force, throwing each piece into the mixer, his face set. He retrieved the dough hook from the floor and fitted it to the machine as he hit the switch so Mabel feared for the safety of his hands. The machine roared into life, hook whirring and twisting, melding fat and flour. He measured in the water – hot, now, so the dough might prove more quickly, though the texture of the bread would be spoiled.

"I'm telling Wills they can keep their business! I'm sick and tired of working for them." He needed to shout above the clamour of the machinery and Mabel could see the anger and knew she must not challenge it. "Don't bother opening up that shop today!"

He took the first batch of bread from the prover, opening the oven doors and throwing the tins to the back to find the best of the heat. "I'm off out once I've finished this."

Mabel left him to his anger, going through to the shop and closing the door behind her, fumbling with the knot of her apron, hands trembling. She saw, through the shop window, the landlord park his car and get out, reaching through to the back seat for the bowler hat and slamming shut the car door before crossing the pavement.

She hid in the safety of the living room as he rattled the handle of the shop door, rapping on the glass and taking his fist to the window. Her heart beating wildly, her legs unsteady, she ran to check the latch was down on the back door, turning the kitchen light off and taking a chair to the windowless alleyway so she might sit where she could not be seen. She prayed the children would not wake. Elbows on knees, hands covering her face, she heard the raised voices in the bakehouse, Frank's cursing, a crash of metal tins hitting the stone floor, more shouting, then silence. The slam of a door. The roar of a car engine.

It was eight o'clock. She measured out the porridge, set bowls on the table, took John from his cot and changed his nappy, rummaging in the dirty washing basket to find Joyce's PE kit because it was a Friday.

Sarah fed the baby his breakfast and sorted the little ones' clothes, wordless apart from asking her mother if she could have the two shillings for the week's dinner money, quickly reassuring her mother it didn't matter when Mabel went to her purse and found it empty.

"Don't worry, Mummy, I'll take it Monday."

"Yes," said Mabel, "tell them you forgot."

It was a blessed relief once the girls set off for school and she could take a quiet moment to think. She settled the little ones on the floor to play, boiling the kettle to make tea and perching upon the edge of a chair with the warmth of the teacup in her hands for comfort. She thought about what she must do. The bakehouse had been silent since Clack left, Frank starting the van up to drive away. The order, then, might at least get to Wills. They paid in pound notes.

She drained her cup and finished the washing-up from breakfast, leaving the porridge saucepan to soak. She fetched tea chests and crates, stowed away in the outside lean-to all these months past, and gathered up newspapers left strewn upon the dresser. She took her best china from the pantry, nestling it between folds of linen as she packed it in a wooden crate labelled "oranges". Then cutlery, rolling pin, toasting fork. Babies' bottles. Bibs and nappies. She emptied the shelves of the kitchen cabinet, tipping tealeaves down the sink, leaving it to stain and discolour because it no longer mattered, and rinsing the teapot under the tap. As she dried it with a cloth she heard Frank come back through the shop.

"That's it then, Mabe," he shrugged off his jacket, reaching into a pocket for cigarettes and matches. "We tried our best, and it didn't pay."

"Where did the money go, then, Frank?" Her voice was scarcely more than a whisper. "We've both worked so hard."

He met her gaze for a moment, stepping over the children's toys scattered about the floor and reaching up to take the pots and pans from the top of the cabinet, passing them to her so she might put them in a box.

"Sometimes things work against you, Mabe. And Clack is taking advantage – he won't wait for his money."

"We need some more boxes, then," she said. "I'll make a start on the upstairs."

"That's my girl," said Frank, almost cheerily. "We've got 'til tomorrow to get out. I've found us a house not too far away, and someone gave me a good price for the van so I've paid a week's rent. Something will turn up. I'll go and fetch some flour sacks for the bedding."

Mabel heard the crashing of tins on the stone floor of the bakehouse, the dull thud of, perhaps, a machine being tipped and rolled, the slamming of oven doors against a brick wall. A sea fret of flour dust drifted through the alleyway into the kitchen and she knew her husband had found a way to vent his anger.

Frank came through to the shop with a paintbrush and bucket to whitewash the windows against the curiosity of the neighbours.

"I'm going round to George and Doreen's," he told her, using the handle of the paint brush to shatter the shelves in the window so that crackles of splintered glass became the frosting on yesterday's custard tarts. "He's lending me the van to move our stuff tomorrow and anyway, he owes me some winnings from the weekend."

When Frank had gone and silence descended, Mabel stood at the counter for a few moments in the half light, picturing the customers who had become so familiar to her, so much a part of her life here. Mr Crowther, who lived alone and had lost a son called Geoffrey in the last days of the war. He'd been eager to show her a photograph of a smiling boy in RAF uniform with pale hair and crooked teeth and Mabel had told him how like his father the boy was – a sandwich loaf and two currant buns, twice a week. Mrs Withers, two Russian slices and a split tin every Friday. Mrs Dunn, a burnt cottage loaf freshly baked and delivered in time for breakfast. Mrs Gardener, six vanilla slices every Thursday morning for her knitting group ("Do you have a box, Missus? So much nicer to serve them from a box, don't you think?"). Mrs Smith, her husband left crippled after an air raid on the corset factory, she coming in every Saturday asking for a penny off a loaf because she managed on a pension. Miss Lesley, a spinster of middle years who taught at the infants' school and had a Victoria sandwich put by every other Tuesday for when her mother came to tea.

Mabel would miss them. All of them. She wondered if they would miss her.

16

Bristol, 2020

On a Tuesday in late June my sisters and I go in search of Lincoln Street, visiting what remains of roads obliterated by the progress of sixty years; neighbourhoods where once mothers tried their best to make homes for their families in streets pockmarked by war.

Lincoln Street does not exist in the same way it did in 1956. Bulldozers have refashioned the streets so that now one melds into another, original thoroughfares unrecognisable. Terraces of stone-built houses have been wiped away in a preference for low-rise apartment blocks and "settlements", maisonettes favouring the rental market and social housing for refugees fleeing faraway lands my parents had never heard spoken of.

We are a stone's throw from where the railway line once threaded its way through the city from station to station, the trains long gone. I park the car in the place where Sarah believes Lincoln Street used to be. There is a double yellow line but we are hoping it's the traffic warden's day off.

"I don't remember much about this house at all." I switch off the engine and reach for my bag at Joyce's feet.

"Just as well," Sarah says from the back of the car. "We just remember the silences for days on end when they didn't speak, or the shouting at night when we hid under the blankets, or the fight with the carving knife when Grampy came to collect his winnings and Frank had reinvested them at the bookies!"

Same old story, I want to say, let's not bother.

My sister buttons her coat, shouldering her bag as we step from the car. "Let me just show you this before we go . . ." She has found a book on post-war Bristol. "Have a look at this." She hands it to Joyce, the page open to a black-and-white photograph. "A Lincoln Street party to celebrate the Coronation! It's a real picture of community, isn't it?"

I come round to look over their shoulders. And it most certainly is an illustration of community: wooden trestle tables set the length of the street, mothers in floral blouses and party hats secured with elastic under chins, young girls in pretty dresses and little boys in white shirts and flannel shorts, clean-shaven men in cloth caps, cigarettes dangling from their mouths. Sandwiches and cakes and buns are piled high on plates and platters of every shape and size for what must have seemed a proverbial feast after the austerity of war-time rationing.

"Well, look at the terraces of houses. It must have been so easy to get to know your neighbours. And the Coronation such a lovely excuse to celebrate together!" Joyce turns the page but there is only the one photograph of Lincoln Street.

"Just like us at Mrs Newson's!" agrees Sarah.

I see in my sisters the desperation to turn for good these memories of family life in the 1950s, but in truth I've learned it was a world we were never fully a part of.

"Let's go, then." says Sarah. "Can I just put this book back in the car? We can look at it again later if you like, when we go for tea."

The street is a concrete mix of 1960s and '70s architecture, front doors built directly at the pavement edge, just as they were two generations before, only now they are made of grey steel and are shut tight against any thought of social mingling. There is a code required for entry. The pavements are deserted, no cars at the kerb in deference to parking restrictions, no sign of a window opened to a summer breeze or a doormat slung across a sill to be aired, no housewife in curlers and hairnet scrubbing a front step. There are no clues, here, to help us imagine the shape of a community.

I can see they doubt it was ever so. It's too hard to watch the disillusionment because I think my big sisters were excited to show me the remnants of a place where our father's business was, for a short time, such a success.

"I really wish I could see the shop window where John and I sat in the pram for hours on end." I'm hoping to remind them of something we can smile about. "Because of that photograph!"

"Oh my word!" says Joyce, and she is smiling, "You were out there for hours. And you not even strapped in!"

"I was obviously very well-behaved."

My sister points to a building at the far end of the street. "Sarah, do you think that's the same pub where our father used to take Grampy for a drink? Before the awful fight with the carving knife?"

It's a dreary building of red brick, windows boarded up and front wall defaced by generations of graffiti, words that make no sense to the uninitiated. It is waiting, I think, for demolition to put it out of its misery.

"I'm not sure this is Lincoln Street at all!" declares Sarah, hanging back as we reach the corner. "I think we're in the wrong place entirely."

We go for tea and cake at the gastropub near Joyce's house. It's almost rush hour and if I leave now I can get to the motorway before the commuters – but I know I must stay until we begin to come out of the morass that is remembering life in 1956.

Joyce goes to the counter to order more tea. I see she is chatting to the lady behind the bar – Joyce is a regular here. The lady is smiling and nodding at something Joyce has said. My sister is known.

Conversation with Sarah finds its way to the tea party and though I'm glad we have something cheerful to turn our minds to, talk of it brings the reality of my responsibility to make it happen. To create happiness when all the foundations of the "reasons why" are of darkness and neglect.

"Let's meet up with Shirley again," I suggest, recognising the convenience of delaying tactics, "and have a look round the Village Club. See what the facilities are like."

"It's only right, isn't it, to celebrate Mabel with tea and cake!" Sarah is huddled over her empty teacup, coat still on and buttoned to the neck. "I'll email Shirley. When shall we go?"

Joyce comes back to sit with us at our table near the window. She's brought cake, a mass-produced affair and nothing at all to remind us of the fondant fancies and Battenberg cakes that our clever father created, day in and day out.

A steady drizzle is pattering at the glass and I'm thinking how miserable it will be, driving for two hours up the motorway in semi-darkness. I have a busy day coming up – a Buckingham Palace garden party to celebrate our support of the Child Bereavement Trust – and it would have been nice to be home early.

We plan our next trip on the journey through Mabel's life. We have a little over twelve months before the centenary of her birth, by which time our project was to be finished. Sarah is eager to visit Clevedon, where we all remember the joy of living near the sea and I recall it was always summer – but the next trip in our timeline is St Anne's, where John and I had scarlet fever and our father went to prison for rates arrears left behind at the bakery, so I can't believe that will be a cheerful visit.

I get up to leave, before the optimistic mood around the table has an opportunity to change.

"Guess where I'm going to tea, tomorrow!" I say, knowing they never will.

The journey home takes three hours instead of the usual two, the motorway grey and murky with spray. I think back to our day together, fascinated they hold such memories of family life that I shared but recall so little of. I only have a memory of adventuring with my sisters.

They are taking me out – just me, not John, so I'm feeling like I'm very special. Nine-year-old Joyce carries me; I'm bunched up awkwardly in her arms, not held close as a mother might but clamped to her swivelled hip rather as a lump of baggage she has been told to take out of the way for a while.

My clothes are all of a heap and I'm clinging on with clenched fists to the lime green wool of her jumper. I am a little afraid of the danger of falling, but big sister Sarah strides on ahead and she is in charge so I have the promise of safety, right there.

We walk and walk, along pavements I've only before seen from my pram, passing ladies I recognise because they are customers and I meet them in the shop when Mummy serves them. Sometimes they stop to speak with us as John and I sit in the pram outside the bakery shop window.

We pass a public house and Joyce, breathless now from the weight of me, nods in that direction, telling me that's where Daddy takes Grampy for a drink. "And can you please stop wriggling?" she implores. "Or else I'm going to drop you!"

We come to the green railings bordering the park with the swings. I'm disappointed for a moment when Sarah doesn't stop, because I thought this was where we were heading. She's striding on ahead and we follow.

"Which gate shall we use?" Joyce asks our big sister, the ringleader, and Sarah turns for a second.

"Barrow Road," she tells us. "Come on – it's just across the bridge."

We've come this way before, when they've been pushing me and John in the pram, and I've seen the steam belching in swirling grey clouds of coal dust that billow over the parapet and fill my mouth with bitterness, grit like burnt toast on my tongue. I'm expecting the piercing scream of the locomotive's whistle but even though I know it's coming, it always makes me jump in fright.

Until today I hadn't noticed the gate in the wall, and now Joyce has stopped and Sarah is looking at me with a serious face as she lifts the latch at the top. No one speaks for a moment and we all watch, enthralled, as the gate swings wide on its hinges; a gang of three daring to disobey. And there it is, far below, the magical place that is the railway track.

Sarah says, "You mustn't ever tell!" in a very stern grown-up voice, and I nod, thrilled, because it seems like this is a big-girls' adventure and here I am, with them, sharing in it.

She reaches to take me from Joyce and, clasping me very tightly against her so two sisters become as one, we begin the descent of the steps. They are fashioned of red brick, narrow and very steep, hugging the wall, no handrail and stretching all the way down, down, down to the railway line far below. Joyce closes the gate behind us.

My eyes are smarting, nostrils burning with the intensity of gritty smoke which threatens to choke, and I press my face into my sister's shoulder, screwing my eyes shut and trying not to breathe. Each step she takes jars, my teeth clenched tight together. The wool of her jumper is scratchy on my face but it smells of vanilla and freshly baked bread, warm and familiar. This, then, is how I am to learn all about adventuring.

It seems such a long descent onto the grass below, which isn't at all green as it should be but smudged tarry black. Sarah holds me more tightly so the breath is squeezed out of me as she takes one long, jerky stride across to the shingle where the steel of the rail glints silver in the sunlight. It continues way into the distance, a connection to faraway places we will never see and cannot imagine.

I hang on to my sister, hands clasped tightly around her neck. It feels dangerous, though I'm not sure why because all is quietness around us. I can just hear the muffled roar of traffic crossing the bridge way above our heads; a world away because we are down here, in this secret and forbidden place.

"Look!" Joyce points, leaping across the shingle to join us. "There's a train in the station. Let's walk along the track and see!"

And I do look, as she says, and the station building with its red-brick walls and green-tiled roof seems so very, very far away. Like a model fashioned from my big sisters' Bako sets.

We set off, Sarah holding me more lightly now, zigzagging back and forth between rail and shingle. I hear the hiss and spit of steam and the ear-piercing screech, metal on metal, of wheels grinding on steel.

I have never told. My sisters have no memory of taking me to the track but I remember it as clear as day. The sight of those steps going way, way down onto the railway line, the acrid smell of black smoke, the scream of the whistle, the feeling of imminent, forbidden danger. I was safe with my sisters and it was a thrilling adventure.

Now we have more staid escapades together – we visit the Shetlands, windswept and barren in late October, to enjoy Joyce's birthday tea in Victoria's Teashop, the northernmost cafe in the UK. I have rung ahead and the dear lady has strung pretty vintage bunting across from corner to corner, so it feels like a real celebration.

We book a table by the rocky shore of Green Island and order fish and chips, Sarah's choice, in the southernmost restaurant in Great Britain. We stroll through a sleepy Cornish fishing village on a warm September evening, watching the antics of oystercatchers at low tide, climbing perpendicular streets to hear 1920s jazz played in an ancient and dusty church hall. St Mawes, my most favourite village by the sea.

We sail on a small ship to the Channel Islands to read books that never speak of trauma, and walk and talk together, breathing clean, sharp air that's blown clear across the Atlantic Ocean and meets us where the surf pounds granite cliffs in a moment of beauty.

Sisters, enjoying the simplest of things in the company of one another; the creation of community. An accidental legacy of a shared and precious connection, inherited without intention by motherless daughters.

17

Bristol, 2020

If ever there were a quiz challenging contestants to recall the addresses of where they had once lived, we would win hands down.

"Perhaps it was just our generation of children," suggests Sarah, in the back of the car as usual and leaning forward between Joyce and me to peer through the windscreen at the house across the road. "Perhaps they were always afraid we would get lost and made us memorise the names and numbers!"

"We were only here five minutes," Joyce reminds us.

The house is terraced and fitted with cheap double-glazing, mid-century triple bay and elegant cornerstones of its neighbours now obliterated in favour of a single flat pane. Net curtains are strung asymmetrically across its width, a weak November sun reflecting off the fake glass in the whiter-than-white plastic of the front door.

"There's the wall we used to sit on to do our knitting!" exclaims Sarah from the back seat. "The lovely lady at the draper's put it by for us, do you remember Joyce? And we bought an ounce a week and knitted slowly to make it last!"

"Mine was light blue with a fleck in it," says Joyce proudly, she who taught me – once I was old enough – to knit, row by painstaking row, translating abbreviations and transcribing instructions in longhand, line by line, so I could cross them through with a pencil as I turned my knitting from hand to hand to begin again.

"Mine was a dark-blue fleck," Sarah recalls, and I glimpse the precious connection between one little sister and another that made the world a safer place.

The red-brick walls and black capstones that my sisters speak of meet together at a simple metal gate that stands open, leaning to one side. I recall the sound of the squeaky hinge, the noise of metal on metal as it clanged shut. From my sickbed on the top floor I knew it was the doctor on his daily visit and I should do as Mummy said straight away and hide my dummy under the pillow so she might not be shamed. At the age of three or four, I knew the rules of how to keep the world from knowing what was happening behind closed doors.

"It's starting to rain, I'm afraid." Joyce sits back in her seat so I can see more easily over her shoulder. "Let's not get out yet."

On the opposite side of the road to number fourteen is a huge monolith of a church hewn from Victorian stone, grey and with a multi-faceted slate roof. A concrete yard between gravestones and outer wall might once have been a garden.

"That's where our mother was married. Do you remember?" Joyce turns to her sister in the back seat. "Our cousin Jeanette once told us how pretty Mabel looked on her wedding day!"

If I had been here by myself, I would have gone inside to make the imaginings more real.

"And that side street is where Auntie Frances's car was parked. Here on the corner! The day she came to give our mother the money to get him out of prison. We watched them from the upstairs window."

"Oh that car!" says Sarah, wistfully. "A shooting brake! Varnished wood round the windows and red leather seats and everything! Do you remember, Joyce? We thought they were so posh!"

"Well, they were," her sister replies, smiling. "And I so, so wanted a ride in that car! But they just talked with our mother on the doorstep then got back in and drove off!"

"Well I don't have many memories of this house, but I *do* remember being in bed for weeks on end with the scarlet fever and then our fun in the garden when I got better, running through long grass in and out of the trees, picking plums to stew over a campfire. There were lots of wasps. You were so good to include me in those adventures. Four-year-olds aren't always a blessing to have around!"

"She gave us an old frying pan. It must have been coming into autumn, because the plums were ripe. We didn't have any sugar but they were sweet enough. Perhaps they were Victorias." Sarah fidgets in her seat, taking off her coat. She has no intention of stepping out.

"Our mother knew a hundred different recipes for plums and pears!" says Joyce, in a jokey kind of voice so we might be spared the pain of remembering how awful that time was – because although it still happens in families now, it's never alright for children to be half-starved and mothers to be worried sick about where the next meal might come from.

"If you go down to the end of the road," Sarah leans in close to my shoulder so I can smell the fragrance of conditioner on her hair, cut short now so it suits her much better, "I'll show you the shop that used to be a post office. That's where Mummy sent me to post the letter to Daddy, and I saw it was addressed to Horfield Prison."

She leans back again so I can only glimpse her face in the rear-view mirror. It is blank. "If you turn the corner at the bottom I'll show you where I had to go to ask the National Assistance for money."

She is thirteen again, doing all she can to help her mother so the world might be set to rights.

"Is there *any* part of your life here that you weren't ashamed of?" It's hard to keep exasperation from my voice.

"Auntie Frances and Uncle Robert!" Joyce clips her seat belt. "She was wearing that beautiful fox fur round her neck . . . do you remember, Sarah?"

We drive to the corner as directed by Sarah, and though I pull up at the kerb I leave the engine running so she knows she is safe.

"I cried all the way home," she says, casually, as though it doesn't matter. "Usually it was Mummy who left, but now it was him who'd gone."

I had hoped that being here together, in the safe place that is my car, we would be able to see the shame for what it really was – an inheritance brought about by the actions and irresponsibility of others and not at all the fault of five little children.

"Well don't forget I had to go to a school friend's house and ask her mother if she had any shoes they didn't want, that I could wear to school!" Joyce winds up the window. "We can go home this way if we turn left at the bottom."

I can see my sisters are relieved to be stepping back into the present. The past is only palatable in small doses.

"Where shall we go next week?" We head out onto the dual carriageway. "We're only halfway through, I think. It's not worth going to Westbury, you said. Where we moved next. The row of cottages has gone now."

"We were only there a couple of months," says Sarah, a bitter edge to her voice. "We didn't even start in a school, I don't think."

And we are all remembering that at thirteen she was awarded a scholarship for the prestigious Bristol Commercial School, there a matter of weeks before he moved us on.

"Eaton Bray," suggests Joyce, her tone light. "Our mother was happy there."

"Well, we'll need to go via the awfulness of Luton," Sarah replies, and I wonder, not for the first time, how we can somehow turn this project around so it might redeem, and not overwhelm.

We are spared the trip to Bedfordshire, at least for the time being. The pandemic has taken hold and the country is in another lockdown. It's hard to check on who is well and who is struggling.

I want to remind Sarah that although we have lived through hard times together – and she suffered more than I – there are adventures ahead for us, and we will always have each other.

I bake six perfect, individual plum crumbles with a sprinkling of Demerara sugar. I wrap each dish in film, packing them carefully into a cardboard box and cushioning them with bubble wrap my husband brings home from the company warehouse, a giant roll the size of a water butt. Astonishingly, it weighs nothing at all.

I label the box in bold black lettering: "St Anne's Plum Crumble." I secure the top with brown tape and address it to my sister.

18

Luton, 1958

"Luton? Why on earth Luton?!" Mabel couldn't get her mind around it, startled as she was by the suddenness of the plan to go. "Though heaven knows, anything is better than staying here." She bent over a box of blankets to press the lid closed so he could tape it down. "But Frank, I don't even know where that is . . . !"

Frank continued in his task of packing up the kitchen cupboards. "It's over near Dunstable."

"Well I've never heard of that either," faltered Mabel, glad to be going, glad that Frank had a plan and had shaken himself into some kind of action – but *Luton*?

"It's a bit of a drive, let's leave earlyish tomorrow." He taped up one box and began on another.

Five hours after setting off they turned into a narrow little street with tired-looking terraced houses either side, and bits and pieces of rubbish scuttling about the gutters. A feral dog rooted through a dustbin. They parked up. Frank went back and forth with boxes and bags, the children trailed behind her as she searched for bread, jam, a half packet of biscuits.

"I'm taking Sarah for an interview tomorrow," he said. "A junior office job. It's not worth her while starting back at school."

A few months later and without warning they left, moving across the main road to the other side of town.

"Is it going to be better there then?"

"I've found another job – one that suits me better. They've offered me a house."

They packed up the van, more randomly now than before, and ushered the children into the back. It was little more than a five-minute drive.

"Up a steep hill off the main road, turn right and up another hill and number fifteen is on the left-hand side." Frank repeated the directions given to him by his new boss.

Mabel saw that it was as grey and dismal as the first; three storeys high and five steps up to the front door. The only difference was the steepness of the hills.

She began to stumble every morning climbing the stairs to rouse Joyce for school and Sarah for work. Mabel guessed the move must have worn her out; it was a challenge to get back up those hills from the shops pushing Cath and John in a double pushchair weighed down with groceries.

"It must be my age," she thought, her monthlies having stopped some time before. "The Change must be coming." She hoped to goodness she wasn't in the family way – that would be the very worst of news.

She bought herself a tonic from the chemist – Sanatogen Wine, highly recommended in an advertisement she saw in *The News of the World*. She ditched her smart black court shoes and wore brown lace-ups with sensible heels. She sat on a chair to do the ironing and sent Frank to buy a large sack of potatoes from the market so the daily shopping trip was more manageable.

"Frank, these stairs will be the death of me!" she told him one evening a few months in, collapsing exhausted onto a chair at the kitchen table, head in hands, while Frank finished his tea.

He took up his overalls for work. "I'll sort some carpet at the weekend," he said, collecting together cigarettes, matches and newspaper. "That will make it easier on your legs."

It was a little easier, Mabel realised, because the carpet meant she could crawl her way to the top of the stairs on her hands and knees.

19

Luton, 2020

I drive to Luton alone, intermittent lockdowns a complication for travellers and, anyway, it's less than an hour from me and in the opposite direction from Bristol.

I sit in my car outside a house where my four-year-old self once lived, not intending to step out; rather, I press the lock on the doors.

I'm grateful I've come by myself, bruised by watching my sisters walk through their past. It's not what I intended when we set out on this project – Frank still doing damage though he is long gone.

The street is narrow, sloping steeply up from the town centre; terraced housing rises to three storeys on either side, the one I've come to find on a bend halfway along. I can imagine the challenge my mother faced in toiling up from the shops each day, two toddlers in a cumbersome 1950s double pushchair, groceries stashed beneath.

Today there is no sign of life, testament, perhaps, to the partial lockdown. Kerbs are overcrowded with cars and vans, nothing too new; the usual wheelie bins litter pavements. Street lamps are lit, weirdly, as it's eleven o'clock in the morning. A light rain is falling and, in time, obscures the view through my windscreen. I could flick the wipers on but I've learnt all I need to know. I take just a few moments to look up at the dormer window of the attic; the frame is rotten and hasn't seen a coat of paint for some years. A pigeon sits on the gable. I wonder if my mother ever looked out upon the street below when she hid up there, fashioning for herself a refuge from the day to day; remembering how to do "fun" with her girls.

"Everything had to be ready," Sarah messages me when she hears I am visiting Luton, "so that every night we could go up to the attic and switch on to Radio Luxembourg the minute it crackled into life at seven o'clock and there she would be, singing along to the latest Ricky Nelson, Buddy Holly and Anthony Newley. Where she found the badminton racquets from I'll never know!"

Joyce joins our digital conversation. "It was our secret place, after you little ones were put to bed. No one ever invited our father – I don't think he ever knew about the badminton net."

"Clive never came home when we lived there. Too far to fetch him."

I drive down the hill and across the High Street to the second house he moved us to. The narrow road is crammed full of parked cars and, again, abandoned dustbins, some smeared in poorly scribed numbers. The road is steep, front gardens sacrificed to carports.

I start the engine, put the car into gear and drive away.

Eaton Bray is a short drive from Luton, through the redeveloped and more respectable parts of the town and way across the Dunstable Downs. I wonder if Mabel's spirits lifted as Frank drove them out through the suburbs and into the wide open spaces. I wonder if my mother's heart grew hopeful.

Any evidence of our family having lived in this village has long been obliterated. Where the boss's pigs wallowed in the mud behind a weathered grey-stone wall there are houses with neat lawns, wooden gables framing each porch. Wheelie bins are tucked under tidy wooden shelters beside tidy front doors and I'm sure no one here keeps chickens.

And no one has named their house "The Piggeries", like Mr Dooley, so I have no way of guessing where our garden might lie beneath the foundations; that wild expanse where John and I pedalled trikes along cinder paths while our mother watched our fun, and we girls stalked each other and laid tracks, and played five stones and hopscotch;

where our mother stood to take a photograph, Joyce's arm around my shoulder, our hair washed and brushed and held back in tortoiseshell slides, gymslips neatly pressed.

The wall around the housing estate looks out of place – too ancient by far – and I feel it must be here, the garden where we picked colanderfuls of our daddy's peas for dinner, shelling them with thumbs and filling our mouths with plump sweetness. Where a hundred chickens pecked and clucked, their fate the cooking pot.

My mother would most certainly have glanced across the High Street to the red-brick farmhouse standing in its gardens of apple trees and lavender. Did she know the lady who lived here? Did she smile and wave as she passed by on her way to school and call out, "Lovely day! Spring is on its way!" Proud of her little one, proud of her garden, proud of what she had made of herself?

I won't find any lingering trace of Mabel here, but I look long and hard at every feature, every house, every hedgerow that her gaze would surely have rested upon. I make my way down School Lane and know that she walked here with me on my first day in school; perhaps she held my hand. Perhaps we chatted together, she and I.

I text my sisters to tell them I am sitting in my car in Eaton Bray. That I haven't found the house, but the shop where they paid tuppence for Jammie Dodgers is still there and the school; and The Mead where we played as children.

"That was a happy place," Sarah messages me. "You don't really notice your mother. She'll have your dinner ready when you get home and your clothes will be washed and ironed and back in the drawer, but you never wonder what thoughts go through her head."

"I've done quite a lot of wondering today," I reply. "Some of it probably fanciful!"

"That was where I joined the Guides for two weeks," replies Joyce. "And Sarah and me were given a bantam each for a pet – Blackie and Ginger – and we found out one Sunday we'd just eaten them for dinner!"

I drive home, realising my house is but twenty miles from Eaton Bray, the bridge that spans the two the expanse of two generations. It has brought unbelievable change to my circumstances. I cannot decide if it is simple fate or the determined ambition of a girl to escape; to run, so she might find a new path in life that is all her own . . . much as my mother did before me.

20

Clevedon, 2020

My sisters and I are visiting Salthouse Fields today, in Clevedon, Somerset. It is soon to be Mabel's birthday and Sarah has suggested we come to where Mabel spent happy months, near the sea.

This is where I remember my mother being well, striding out as she pushed my little brother in the pushchair, smiling and happy as she walked us to the park. I remember it being always sunny.

Clive was home from school a good deal, so it was possibly the summer holidays. I fell in the goldfish pond in a neighbour's garden in my favourite dress – it must have been that we were allowed out to play with little friends in the road, something my mother had often, in the past, been heard to say was "common".

The weather in July can be disappointing, but today is bright and warm. I park the car outside the house where we once lived and we gather coats (which we three sisters are never without) and bags, setting out on the walk from Strude Road to the beach. We are making for what was once the Haven Cafe, where Mabel had a little job and earned her own money.

"This is the way she would have walked." Sarah sounds confident, as though we are going to find nothing but goodness here.

"It's lovely to think we are retracing her steps in a place where she was happy." Joyce is striding beside me in her usual energetic way – glad, I know, to see our older sister excited about the day. And I'm glad, too; hopeful for a cheerful remembering of happy family times, especially since our conversations after my trip to Eaton Bray. It's possible we might yet be able to turn this story for good.

"We need to pick up the pace," Sarah says. "You know how fast she always walked!"

We agree – our mother would have been hurrying, five children left behind in the care of the eldest, a husband enjoying an afternoon sleep before a night shift, tea left on the table. The anticipation of a few moments to herself coupled with a sense of purpose.

"She was so proud of getting this little job!" Our sister is walking out in front – it's as though she can't wait to be there; as though she is truly expecting to meet our mother as we round the next corner in this place of sunshine and summertime pleasure. "And she loved being near the sea," Sarah continues, "because she suddenly got better when we moved here."

It was remission, of course; my nursing experience tells me that. And "remission" is never to be confused with "healing".

It's a ten-minute walk. I recall the excitement of coming to the playing fields at teatime, John in the pushchair, six-year-old me trotting alongside to keep up, Clive holding onto Joyce's arm, grinning wildly and sensing the happiness of the moment. Perhaps he, too, caught the taste and smell of salty air and sea breezes. His walk was gangly and uncoordinated; he'd never seen it done – just learned that people got from "a" to "b" and sometimes they rushed so a walk became something much more lively.

"We must have moved here in the summer, I think," suggests Joyce. "Do you remember if we were here for more than one school year?"

"The good times didn't last," I hear the resentment in Sarah's voice. "He soon got fed up and started looking for jobs again. Once *The British Baker* started coming through the letterbox, we knew we were on the move."

"This was where I went to the junior school in the morning," Joyce says. "Walked home for dinner, went back in the afternoon and was told to get myself along to the senior school, I was too old!"

Oh goodness. Did my poor eleven-year-old sister have to go through that humiliation all by herself?

Because I drive the car that brings us to these places of remembrances, I feel the responsibility of minimising the damage. It feels like we take one step forward and two back. Finding something we can be glad about, or grateful for, is proving an impossibility; there is always a chaser of regret.

"Let's find the Haven Cafe," I suggest. "You told me she loved working there. Her first proper job."

"Oh, yes!" agrees Sarah, cheerfulness regained. "She loved that little job!"

"Was she a cook?"

"Oh, no," she says. "Nothing that grand, I'm afraid. It was a three-hour shift every weekday night, taking the eyes out of potatoes."

"She got the sack," Joyce states, boldly. "It wasn't her fault. That was the night Clive had a fit in the garden and fell in the stingers, and Sarah sent me to run all the way from home to get her. I'd never crossed a busy road by myself before. She got the sack the next day."

"That wouldn't be allowed, nowadays!" I say, the co-owner of a company with two thousand staff.

Salthouse Fields come into view, trees on either side in full leaf, dappled sunshine of midsummer blinding and shading in turn as we cross the avenue. No fence around the green so it remains open to all, though now the playground is bordered by a metal railing.

The miniature train is there, just as I remember; a painted sign tells us it runs only at weekends and school holidays and the rides are no longer thruppence. I text my husband; he takes just a few seconds to calculate that the fare has increased by three hundred and thirty-six times since the 1960s.

"That's where you fell off and cried your eyes out, so we had to go home!" Joyce is pointing at the swings. She is eleven years old again and it feels as though she hasn't forgiven me.

The expanse of green is as long and wide as I remember, but it is less grassy – more moss and weeds than public lawn. Perhaps it always was; why would a five-year-old either notice or care. The Haven is renamed but a cafe still, a stone's throw from the sand and a half mile from the pier. It is an Edwardian home converted into a cafe – perhaps once with an ambition to be more, but now part of a national chain of fast-food restaurants. Standing in its own grounds it has a flagstone patio set about with wooden chairs and tables, overlooking the sea; what were once most probably gardens and shrubberies are now a tarmacadam parking lot for customers not prepared to walk the few steps from the public car park.

We skirt the building in search of the entrance.

"Are we buying lunch here?" Sarah asks as we finally find the front door, closed so it might deter any customer who might want to enter but not locked, so she turns the handle and we step into the gloom.

"Let's look at the menu, shall we?" Joyce suggests.

The place is deserted. We can't find a menu.

"Shall we just buy takeaway coffees, do you think?" she asks. "It doesn't look very lively."

"I'll pay," says Sarah. "It's my turn."

"There's a bench – over by the swings." I long to be back out in the sunshine. "I'll go over and save us a seat."

I head off towards the playground, glad to be able to breathe clean, cool air, marvelling that I last walked this way so very long ago; back when we were a little family of children who laughed and played and jostled together and believed that the world might, at last, have found us a place to settle, here by the sea.

The rhythmic sizzle of surf on shingle is just a step or two away, over the wall. I lean on the crackled white paint of the metal railing and close my eyes for a moment, picturing the child I was, five years old and sitting on a swing in a park which is bordered by a road yet sits at the very edge of the Atlantic Ocean. Like it's lifted from the pages of a picture book.

I feel the wooden seat beneath my bare legs, warm from the sunshine of an August day, the shift of the chains beneath my fingers, the soft, sweet air on my freckled face carried on breezes fresh blown in from the Americas. My brothers and sisters are with me. We are complete. I am wearing a dress of yellow gingham, inherited from my big sister. It is my favourite.

The grass is green, the wide, wide Somerset sky a dusky blue and my mother is set behind me, pushing me up, up into the world of the seagulls. She is happy, smiling, laughing out loud as my little brother John, in the baby seat beside me, kicks his chubby legs and squeals in delight at this adventure. A skyward freedom mixed with a glorious sprinkling of danger.

And I am flying . . . higher and higher as my mother dares me to be frightened; and when I reach the pinnacle of my flight I see the sparkly blue-green of the sea, taste the saltiness of surf in my mouth – and my smile is fixed by the rush of air upon my face, and I can hear, from a land far, far beneath me, the laughter and summertime happiness of children building kingdoms of castles and turrets on the seashore beyond the wall. And I am all alone in the blue, blue vastness between earth and sky, and nothing can touch me or hinder my joy. And I look below, as I begin to fall, and fall, and I can no longer see over the wall to the world of happy families because my mother has ceased pushing. I glance behind me and she isn't smiling now, but checking her wristwatch and halting the flow of John's swing in a jagged wrench, a cruel twisting of the chains which gave him flight. He yells, but protest is in vain.

And I am falling, falling, and there is nothing I can do but scuff my feet to stop, feeling the scrunch of gravel beneath my sandals. My mother is lifting her baby boy from the swing and she takes my hand to jump me off the seat. Her face is still. It is time to go home. She does not want to go.

I hear my sisters chatting together as they bring coffees and I take a moment, before they are too close, to unlatch the gate, pushing it open on a reluctant hinge, crossing to where the swings hang on rusty chains. Empty of laughing children now, the playground that is here is not at all the place I remember. Not the place where, for a handful of moments, my mother and I shared a simple joy.

"Oh, please let the swing seat be the very same one I sat upon when I did not know God had safer days ahead for me!"

21

The Channel Islands, 2020

A marsh harrier, monarch of the Jersey skies and a male with a wingspan near on two metres, soars on a thermal past a window left open so I might enjoy the glory of an autumn breeze. We meet eye to eye, the great bird and I, he weightless in a cloudless sky, me grounded at a desk littered with scraps of paper and pens of differing colours. An empty teacup. He is the free one – soaring over an island of green fields set in a Prussian blue ocean, nothing to hinder his flight between the two. There are no horizons he cannot explore; no barriers to who he is and what he seeks. He is truly a masterpiece of Nature's engineering, perfectly suited to the world he has been born into.

Not all human babies are born that way; perfect.

This morning, a bright day in early November when the light is clear and sharp, the sun low in the sky so shafts of golden light sparkle on winter webs, I have set myself the task of remembering our brother Clive. I cannot tell the story of my mother's life and wipe him from it, as he was himself in those days of a long-ago family. Today, in my safe place where the past has no foothold, I hover like the marsh harrier over the scene.

22

Bristol, 1961

I am a child on an unexpected outing. I feel special, because my father has chosen me to share his morning. Six-year-olds don't feel remorse at banishing a less than perfect child to an institution; they only assume the world has provided a fair and just solution to disability.

My sisters tell me they never went with their father to take Clive back to Bristol Blind School after the holidays so I can't understand why I did, several times. Perhaps my mother was glad to get me out from under her feet; perhaps I was – momentarily – the daughter who was the latest flavour of the month with our father. Perhaps I was the one who didn't answer back. Perhaps I simply asked if I might go and he didn't care one way or the other.

Mummy sees us off at the door; she hands the small brown suitcase to Daddy. It is the very same one she took as she ran from Blagdon, though now my brother's name is written, freehand, on the chequered cloth of the lining. Our father takes it to the car. Clive is swaying back and forth as he stands ready to go; I suppose he is excited to be returning to school. His chair in the corner of the sitting room has not been the most exciting place to spend eight long weeks.

"Here's your tuck shop money." Mummy touches his hand with her own so he might realise he must grasp the coins. "I'll write every fortnight as usual and send your chocolate bar and half a crown – be sure to keep it safe."

Clive nods, pocketing the money and prancing a little, fingers splayed, head circling in uncontrolled energy like an electric charge has been passed through his body. He is recovered now from the grand-mal seizure he suffered as he dressed – always the epilepsy overcomes him on the day he arrives home from school, repeated on the day he is to return. We know this and are always ready, a ramshackle band of amateur first aiders.

"Will you be coming to Open Day, do you think? I'm playing the piano solo, while the parents have tea in the hall." He prances again, daring to be proud of himself for just a brief moment.

He doesn't see that she is already back inside, taking his coat from the bannister.

"Let's be having you then." Daddy is in a rush to be done with the errand of getting his oldest son back to school so the day can properly begin. He grips the boy's elbow to encourage hurry. "Sure you've got everything? What about all those library books that came in the post over the summer?"

"I've done it!" I pipe up, happy to be thought useful, skipping along behind them as Mummy closes the door on us. "They're already in the boot." They are massive, the RNIB books. And heavy. Weighted down by a necessary volume, each letter punched onto the thick brown paper taking up the equivalent space of two words for any sighted reader.

"Bye, Mum!" he calls, but she is gone, back to the bowl of washing-up she left soaking in the kitchen sink. I admire my brother's courage; we are never brave enough to drop the "Mummy" and "Daddy", we who live amongst them and do not have another place of escape.

We settle into the back seat of the car, well-worn crackled leather hot and sharp against the backs of bare knees. Daddy goes round to the front to crank the starting handle and I watch the vicious wrench on his shoulder as it kicks back, the engine leaping into life with a blast of the exhaust. I wind the window down to let in some air, the inside of the car stale and stifling after three days of September sunshine.

"Do that window up!" my father instructs me as he climbs back into the driver's seat. "It's too blowy."

It's unfair that glorious weather should arrive as we must turn our thoughts to school; over the summer we've moved from the seaside place of parks and playgrounds to a corner shop in the back streets of Bristol. My mother sits up half the night to knit beautiful matinee jackets in intricate patterns, and booties with threaded ribbons of pink or blue, selling them the very next day at her drapery counter so she must knit again, half the babies in the local prams and pushchairs wearing layettes of her creation.

I've seen the way she polishes the glass counter where her work is displayed; I've watched her smile at customers, noting their surprise at the perfection of the handiwork. I've even caught my father looking sideways as she serves the next in line – as though he disapproves of how she is drawing attention away from the opposite corner of the shop where he has set himself up as a gentleman's barber. There is danger in the air when I see this but, at six years old, I can only guess at what it might mean for us in some future moment.

For now, September has brought me worry enough; I am to start at a new school, St Gabriel's. The dread is familiar to me. I must walk to the school gate with my mother, there to be left with a stranger once she has said a quick goodbye and turned for home. I will need to find my way through unfamiliar corridors in search of a toilet, or later seek out the cloakroom where my coat is hanging on a peg which is not yet named, because I wasn't expected here. I will walk into a new classroom with a mismatched uniform, since in Clevedon I wore green – and before that, brown in Eaton Bray, and St Gabriel's children are all in blue. I have no PE kit. Shoes are too small so toes will be cramped by playtime, when no one will want to invite the "new girl" into their skipping game so I will surely stand alone at the edge of the fun until the bell rings again; and because there is no money for school dinners John and I will need to run home and back inside the hour so we are not late in re-finding our classrooms, where we will soon discover whether or not our new teachers are kind.

These things are to come upon us in another day or so but for now I am enjoying the novelty of a drive out in the sunshine, Clive sitting beside me as though we are adventuring together.

"What are you playing on the piano then, at the Open Day?" I ask my big brother, looking out the window because it is never necessary to meet his eye as we speak. I'm marvelling at the privilege he has of playing such a grand instrument from the world of the rich – the world of ballet lessons and friends coming to tea and chestnut ponies with plaited manes, the stuff of Noel Streatfeild and Enid Blyton and Ruby Ferguson; stories I devour with a hungry longing while hiding from my father so he doesn't catch me curled up with a book, when he has been known to snatch it from me and fling it across the room so I stop wasting my time and turn again to whatever work he has presently fashioned for his family to do.

"All the boys have to learn piano, whether they're any good or not," Clive tells me, the car throwing us to one side on the slippery seat so we bump together as my father takes a corner at speed, out onto the main road, gears grinding. "They train us all to be piano tuners."

I find this hard to understand. I have only seen pianos in school halls and never knew they required any kind of attention. "That sounds like a very boring job," I offer, remembering the escapades of Nancy Drew and Timmy the dog. I consider my clever brother, ten years old and an expert on all things cricket-related, and I think about our promise to one another that adventurous days were coming once we were grown-up; certainly more adventurous than any tuning of a piano. "I thought you and I were going to be missionaries together. In Africa."

I hope Daddy can't hear our conversation, as Clive and I have kept this plan a secret. But he is whistling to himself so he probably isn't listening.

Clive turns to the window. A low sun blinks between terraces of stone-built houses so that momentary shafts of bright light cross his face, and I see it is blank. I cannot guess what he is thinking. We've often asked our brother if he can see the difference between light and dark, but he can't tell us. There is no shared language, no common understanding of one thing or another, between the sighted and the blind; of what looks like what. No comparisons possible between the night-time dreams of one child and the mysterious silhouetted shadows of another sleeper who has never seen but only felt.

It's a twenty-minute drive from our house to Bristol Blind School through streets that all look the same to me; flurries of pigeons disturbed from pecking dirt in the gutters by the passing of the car. Town pigeons are a poor substitute for seaside seagulls soaring high above us on a Clevedon beach, the screech of a gawky baby begging food from its mother, the fun of chasing them across the stony sand so they might not steal our teatime sandwiches. I can't imagine there will be any after-school adventures now – not now we live above a shop in Wilton Street where our only entertainment is playing cricket between one pavement and another.

My father turns the car off the busyness of the Bath Road and we are passing beneath an avenue of beech trees. Sunlight dances among the leaves. Shadows play on the car and across my brother's pale face.

"Tell John to remember to listen to the Test Match – we're up against Pakistan." Clive's voice is loud in the quietness of the car.

He and I sway gently from one side to the other as the car takes the curve of the school drive. The tyres swish and swoosh on the gravel; Clive sits up straighter in his seat, leaning forwards, alert. I guess he is looking forward to being back and I'm sad he should prefer to be here at school and not at home to play with me and John. He has recently taught us cribbage, a game which causes no noise and disturbance in the corner of the room where he sits. No one is annoyed by our fun if we keep as quiet as mice and don't cheer as we win.

There is a chaos of cars at the top of the drive where it turns a full circle before the entrance to the school, double doors of heavy oak standing open and a dark void beyond. There are families and boys everywhere so my father curses under his breath as he edges the car between one cluster and another. Big brothers carry stacks of Braille books tied about with string, little sisters struggle with kit bags, fathers guide sons towards the front steps with a hand beneath an elbow. Clive doesn't have a kit bag and I wonder if he will be in trouble, like me. Younger children are running wild, weaving in and out of boys who cannot see the bottom step, so some are tripped. Partially sighted boys are the independent ones; they march up the steps in a straight line and do not falter. They are the boys who, Clive tells me and John, must always be obeyed. They are the secret stealers of tuckshop money and chocolate bars slipped into envelopes by well-meaning mothers.

My father at last finds a space to park, next to the playing field where I last came to watch Clive at sports day. It was a spectacle of controlled madness: gangly boys in too-short shorts and mismatched socks running the length of a track, unmarked, holding on to guide ropes staked between imaginary lanes, heads turned to the right and left but never in the direction they were running so it seemed a miracle when they crossed the finishing line; parents laughing and cheering as their boys broke the tape, hands red-raw from the burn of the rope.

Now the field stands empty of all but goalposts set up for Autumn Term football. I'd once asked Clive how they can play a game when no one can see the ball . . . he told me, "There's a bell in it," adding, "but there's always a lot of crashing into one another." I realised that blindness means a boy must learn to be brave.

The engine sputters to a stop and the handbrake comes up on its ratchet. Daddy opens the door without speaking and goes to collect the suitcase from the boot. I run round to hand Clive his rain mac and, as he steps from the car, my poor brother bumps his head because I forget to remind him to stoop. I notice Mummy has replaced a missing button on the coat, tortoiseshell brown when it needed to be blue. No matter, I can imagine her thinking, he can't see it. I know these small things will indeed matter to a school-room bully.

My father slams shut the boot of the car, taking Clive's elbow to steer him towards the steps. My brother's arm is extended forward, awkwardly, because Daddy is dragging him along, walking with too much hurry for an unsighted boy to be sure of his footing. I carry the mountain of books, steadying them with my chin. We are surrounded by the chatter and laughter of boys and siblings, the sighted ones scampering up the steps, the unsighted feeling for the first with a tentative toe, clinging more tightly to the arm of a chaperone until he passes through the doorway and has a map in his head which keeps him safe.

There is a suffocating stink of stale urine as we take the last step and enter the gloom of the school hall, reminding me of the public lavatories on the seafront at Clevedon. I hold my breath as long as I can. Here in the hall, boys jostle and collide as suitcases are piled inside the door ready for porters to sort into dormitories. The vaulted ceiling of the hall expands and echoes back the shout of one boy to another, the last-minute pleas of fathers to "remember to write", the instructions from teachers robed in black gowns which sweep the floor to "be quick and get yourselves sorted", and from the steps behind me there is the weeping of a small boy for his mother.

"Hey, Clive, have you brought that record you promised me?" It's a sighted boy who has spotted us; I know he is sighted because he is looking straight at Clive – something my brother never does when he speaks to us, because we have never told him that is how conversation is done. Not all learning happens in schools.

"Yes!" my brother yells back, grinning, chin lifting and face animated. "My sister got it for me! Meet you in the Common Room later!"

And I am the disabled now, in this world of Special School. My brother is lost to me; I'm of no help to him in this place of darkness and half light.

"Come on, let's get you in," says my father.

I know he is in a rush to be gone because I heard him tell Mummy he would be calling in on Uncle George on the way back. I guess he will be watching the horse racing and Auntie Doreen is sure to be cross about the intrusion. She always has a grumpy face and never offers me as much as a glass of orange squash – though mostly Daddy leaves me outside in the car for ages until the racing is over and he can drive to the bookies to collect his winnings . . . or not. I know it will matter to Mummy if he has taken what she calls the rent money from behind the clock.

Clive dumps his case in the corner with all the others, tripping over an abandoned kitbag, stopping long enough to turn his head, sideways on and chin up, in my direction. "Don't forget to practise what I taught you. We'll do some more at Christmas. If I come home, that is."

He doesn't always – come home. He goes to somewhere he calls his "other Mummy and Daddy".

During the summer, exiled to his chair in the corner, Clive has been teaching me Braille; I have begun to understand how to clip a silver frame across the width of a page of thick brown paper, how to take the wooden handled dotter and make letters using different formations of dots within the windows of six points that run the length of the frame. I have learned how to write a sentence backwards. I have discovered why my brother has calluses on thumb and forefinger.

"I will – but next time teach me the shortcuts!" I know there are secret symbols which mean I don't have to keep writing "the" and "and" and other annoying repetitions. "It's not fair otherwise!"

There are voices rising and falling all around us, echoes melding together in a melee of "first day back" frenzy, boys of all shapes and sizes dispersing along the corridor towards the staircase which leads up to the dormitories, nothing to soften the noise of two hundred boys returning to school.

The corridor is a gloomy space of high ceilings and green-tiled walls, cardinal-red floor newly stained a dark crimson for the start of the school year. Frosted windows way above my head are uncurtained; naked electric light bulbs suspended on brown flex are not switched on. The thick smell of old urine is stronger here, windows shut tight for eight long weeks while the summer sun warmed the air within.

There is a woman standing guard at the foot of the staircase. I know the woman is the matron Clive speaks of, because she is wearing a dark-blue uniform and a starched white cap and apron. Now her voice comes, shrill as a police whistle.

"No parents allowed further than the hall, if you please! Boys only up the stairs!"

Clive has told us stories about Matron and her so-called nurses, but we are instructed not to believe them. My parents hush him whenever he begins to explain about the cold baths, to describe the leather strap against a wet bottom for no reason the boy could tell, perhaps for an untidy locker or a shoe left scattered upon a floor – for though a blind boy might sweep a splayed hand this way and that in a frantic search beneath his bed, a part-sighted boy may have kicked it out of reach in a moment of spite. Beds are wetted, boys forbidden to visit the toilet after lights out; soiled sheets left to fester and dry to a yellowing crust. Seizures happen in the loneliness of a night dormitory, boys abandoned to recover alone; daytime fits are attended to with a cold spoon prised between juddering teeth, twisted so that tongues may not be bitten and cause recriminations.

We must go. My father takes the monstrous stack of library books and piles them against the wall. We are making our escape. "Don't you let me see those clothes come home in that state again!" he tells his boy in place of the fond farewells other fathers are calling to their sons. "I've never seen such a load of rags. Money doesn't grow on trees, you know. What happened to all those new shirts your mother sent you back with last time?"

My brother doesn't answer, but I remember the stories he tells me about the big boys – the partially sighted ones – and I know the reason.

Clive straightens, turning his face away from his father now, away from me.

"Is that you, Clive?" A shout goes up behind us. "I've brought my new wireless! See you after tea!"

I see my brother grin, hear him shout back, "See you in the Common Room!" And I understand he has changed from being the Clive I know; he has become "one of them". He has no need of us.

"Bye then," I want to say, but I don't because my father has already left the hall and I must follow. I wait long enough to see my brother grinning wildly at nothing in particular, reconnected now with a friend who, like himself, has a love of music. He has discovered a secret place to listen and sing along to the tunes, as Mummy loves to do.

I see it is a precious thing and I wonder if she knows. I'm going to tell her when we get home. I want to be glad for him but I am so very sad to let him go.

I watch Clive put one outstretched hand to the wall, face turned upwards, head turning from left to right as though it has no purpose; he is skimming fingertips along the tiles until he feels the corner where the corridor opens up wide before him. And then, like the others, he runs.

Three decades on, a journalist publishes a memoir about life as a person born blind. He was at Bristol Blind School with Clive and he mentions him by name, especially describing his enjoyment of music and his capacity to memorise lyrics, entertaining the Common Room with his singing.

I buy three copies of the book and post one to each of my sisters.

"Sit somewhere lovely with a cup of tea and read the chapter on Bristol Blind School," I tell them. "It was all true."

Joyce sends a text, late into the night on the same day she's received the book. "There wasn't anything we could have done – it was just the way of things with disability in those days."

Sarah replies, "We should do a headstone for Clive's grave. It was a Council funeral in Torquay cemetery, wasn't it, so it will still just be an unmarked patch of ground."

Oh my goodness. Our mission in life has become one of putting headstones on graves, years after the event. If it weren't so very sad it would be comical.

23

Blagdon, 2020

"You're only allowed three memories each of Wilton Street," I tell my sisters, "otherwise I'm just writing more of the same."

The unimaginable has happened – Connie has sold up and moved Up North to be near her family. A lady of middle years has taken over; she's all of a fluster, though we are her only customers. Sadly, the Formica table has gone – we presume to Connie's new home – and in its place a wooden, rectangular affair crowds the doorway and shrinks the space between customer and counter. Gone, too, the hats and gloves and vintage tweeds. Now the racks are filled with a multi-coloured miscellany, coat hangers hung this way and that. There is the faint aroma of fusty wardrobes that might more usually be found in a charity shop.

"Second-hand clothes," she tells us. "Some of my things I don't need any more."

Oh my goodness. If only successful retailing were that easy.

"I was thirteen," says Joyce, obligingly opening the dialogue as I sit with pen poised. "I passed for The Commercial School but I didn't go – that's just background, mind you, it's not one of my three facts."

I write it all down in one long sentence and put brackets, so as not to upset her.

"I want to mention Dr Ahmed," Sarah says, twirling her coffee cup, keeping her voice low. None of us want the lady to overhear. Close as we are to the counter, we don't yet know if she is the kind of person who will butt in with an opinion. "He was so very kind to our mother. He saw her every week – organised the calliper for her leg so she didn't trip up kerbs and stairs quite so much, and gave her a prescription for a tonic and a pair of elastic stockings. I remember she only had one pair so she had to wash them out in Fairy soap suds every night and hang them over the fireguard to dry."

"It was the right leg that gave her all the trouble," adds Joyce, helpfully.

I'm scribbling everything down in an A4 notebook. I look up. "I broke my arm on the ice in that bad winter of 1961, when snow was piled waist high at the side of the road for weeks. John was chasing me."

"That was after Dad closed the barbershop and drapers and opened up with firewood and coal and coke," says Joyce. "And you had that lovely boyfriend, Sarah, who used to come and help us chop the wood." She is cheating because it's not her "fact" to tell. "He was a soldier."

"Jeremy," answers our sister. "Our father didn't approve of him."

"I got knocked down by a van when we were playing cricket in the street and you were bowling, and you shouted 'RUN!' so I did."

"You should have looked," Joyce replies.

The lady comes to clear the table, so we feel obliged to either pack up our things or order a second coffee. Sarah steps to the counter for more drinks; we are meeting with Shirley but she isn't due for another twenty minutes.

"She tried to leave him while we lived there," I remind them when Sarah comes to sit with us again. "I remember. She had her coat on and they were arguing in the shop. Shouting at one another."

Joyce nods. "Yes, she couldn't have got very far, her walking was too bad. I think she just went for the afternoon."

A seven-year-old hiding in my mother's skirts, I knew fear. Harsh words were flung as insults across the shop. She had a grip on John's hand, but not mine. Two carrier bags of clothes were on the floor at her feet.

"You can have him but you can't take *her*!" he'd yelled, tipping the bag of blouses and vests out onto the floor. She went without answering; without fighting for me, a mix of being thought worth keeping and not worth keeping at all, rolled into one horrible lump in my throat.

I feel the memory of the fear now but I don't write the story down. Instead I try something less disturbing. "She sat up all night to knit me a pink cardigan to wear to a birthday party."

"He sent me and Sarah down the road to borrow a tax disc from a neighbour's car so he could copy it and alter his old one to match. Then we had to take it back!" Joyce looks as though she enjoyed the escapade.

"I went to St Gabriel's School and sang the solo in the school play, though no one came to watch."

"I bought a Dansette record player with money saved up from my wages and the only record I had was Cliff Richard, 'I Love You'," Sarah tells me.

I remember. We got into trouble for boring our parents with the same song played over and over. I write it down.

"We went to the pictures and took you, Cath. Elvis Presley in *Blue Hawaii.*"

"No," corrects Sarah, "that was when we moved to Stour Road, a bit later."

"Oh, don't count that one then," Joyce says. I cross it through.

"I thought we wouldn't include Stour Road," I tell them. "It was the same old story in a different place."

"And all those lodgers! Really hard work for her." Sarah moves aside so the lady can place the tray on the table; we suspend our conversation.

"Goodness knows where the lodgers came from. All men from a training centre." Joyce hands me a white china mug. Gone are Connie's pretty cups and saucers. "Sarah and I used to take vinegar to bed to dab on the itches. It must have been bed bugs; I know he got the mattresses from the Army and Navy. That place was filthy."

"Well no one could expect her to clean a house three-storeys high, with men in every room expecting this and that! And all those stairs!" Sarah sits forward over her cup.

It's not fair she should feel the need to defend our mother. We are all on the same side.

"Come on, we've gone off track. It's Wilton Street we're doing."

Sarah recovers in the length of time it takes to stir her coffee. "Back to Wilton Street then – he came to find me at work and asked for the money I was given by the manager to take to the bank." Her face is very still. "Mum went to Auntie Edna and asked her to lend it to me so I could take it back the next morning."

"When he started selling firewood and coal," Joyce joins in, "we all had to take turns going to Yatton in the van to collect the firewood and then it all got tipped out on the kitchen floor to be sawn up. We got lots of splinters. You little ones Sellotaped the bags shut! And then at the wholesalers where he went for the coal, he'd have us jump out of the van on the way out so he could fiddle the cost on the weighbridge!"

"Hold on, I can't write that fast . . ."

"I worked the bundling machine so you little ones could bag up the kindling." Joyce takes her tea to the counter; she drinks it black and the lady has added milk to all the mugs. Perhaps she has no milk jugs.

When she comes back to the table I take up my pen to finish off. "You've told me too many things; it's going to be too long a chapter when I wanted to keep it short."

Joyce shrugs but doesn't argue.

"My turn then. I had my twin pram the Christmas we lived there, and my dollies."

"That's four things," says Joyce. "I remember getting a pair of frilly knickers, but they were lost in the Christmas wrappings and I never saw them again!" Such are the disappointments of childhood – six decades later she still looks sad when she tells me.

"Well I think you've lost count altogether, Cath, because it all sounds like a lot more than three each, to me!" Sarah intervenes.

Shirley arrives, so I put my notebook away. She's as cheerful as always, accepting the offer of coffee. Taking her bag from her shoulder she suggests we sit outside. Perhaps she distrusts the lady at the counter.

She has brought copies of the Devon newspaper article that reported Clive's death. The print is black and bold and smudged, like real ink has been used – as it most probably was back in 1975.

"I can't find the ad. from the 'personal column' of the *Bristol Evening Post* that you told me about," she says, "the one that said he'd died, asking for any relatives to come forward. But I'll keep looking, so try and give me a more accurate date."

We pass the newspaper article between us; it's brief, calling our brother "a blind man" when we know full well he was – and always will be – a boy.

"I've managed to find a copy of the inquest report," Shirley says. "I've ordered it, so I'll forward it on to you."

When it arrives in my inbox later in the week, I decide I won't pass it onto my sisters until the next morning when daylight comes. It's too sad to be read last thing at night. Disability should never mean a young man with epilepsy is left unattended to drown in a bath of water.

24

Torquay, 1975

On an overcast, half-light December day that threatened rain, my sisters and I travelled together to our brother's funeral. The cemetery was on the south coast, very near to where he had been living for the previous six years. I made enquiries regarding Clive's body being brought back to Bristol so he could be buried with his mother, but in the unfamiliar world of interment I discovered every crossing of a county boundary must be paid for, and none of us had any money.

After calling in to collect our wreath from the florist we left the city suburbs by nine in the morning for a three-hour drive, with a stop on the way to feed Joyce's baby. We talked very little on the journey; the unthinkable had happened. Our brother, who until three days before we'd thought to be happily settled by the sea – albeit in an old people's home – was dead. And with such little notice of the funeral, we had each left difficulties behind us. Sarah had given three children into the care of a neighbour; Joyce two. I had gone through a harsh interview, compassion being in short supply and student nurses required to drop down a set if their leave overran the allotted days. I had already spent time visiting my father as he went back and forth to hospital for cancer treatment.

No way could I imagine changing sets, to be left behind by my friends; the "belonging" meant too much to me. I had a ticket for the late-night coach back into London, ready for an early shift the following day.

The cemetery in Torquay was not at all by the sea as we had imagined; rather it sat at the edge of a busy through-road bordered by a red-brick wall, skirted with weeds. Long ago there were gates, but now two stone monoliths stood alone to mark the entrance.

Joyce parked opposite, taking the opportunity to change the baby's nappy. As we all sorted coats and scarves from the back of the car, a hearse pulled up at the kerb opposite.

"That must be them," said Sarah. She helped Joyce lug the pram from the boot and settle the baby, the hood pulled up so she might be protected from the damp air. Joyce took an extra blanket from the back seat.

Men in black overcoats stepped out of the hearse, one glancing over the road but not smiling, a second opening the tailgate of the car; others came to help shoulder the coffin. They were chatting together, as though it were just another day – which I supposed it was, for them.

"Let's quickly give them our flowers," I suggested.

Sarah was in time to place the wreath upon the coffin before the men set off, no conversation to be had. I guessed paupers' funerals did not warrant unnecessary niceties.

"That looks better," she said as we fell into step behind the gloomy entourage, "as though somebody cared about him."

Which it seems we didn't, I wanted to say, *because here he was in Devon and there was not one day when we visited, or asked about how he was doing.*

I hadn't noticed a fine drizzle falling until I saw the speckled shoulders of the pallbearers; Joyce bent to tuck the blanket more closely around her baby in the pram. We had not thought to bring umbrellas.

The long walk up through the cemetery, along one path and then another and another, was taken in silence. The men in black overcoats walked quickly – I thought perhaps our brother might weigh nothing at all. Or then again maybe a council funeral must be done and dusted in record time so that subsequent, paying mourners could be given more personal attention.

We passed impressive statues of guardian angels and crosses of sculptured stone. There were flowers on one or two of the graves – some plastic, bleached grey by summer sunshine and winter frosts and left as a token of a life remembered well enough, though not so very well as to warrant the inconvenience of regular visiting to bring fresh roses.

When I had begun to think the walk up through the cemetery would never end, a keen wind freezing our faces, I saw we had reached the farthest point where a brick wall met the edge of a wasteland beyond. There the men stopped at a trench, newly dug, fresh soil piled to one side in readiness for earth to obliterate any evidence that Clive had ever lived and breathed and mattered in the world. Sarah, walking beside me, gave a little gasp. Perhaps she was remembering our mother's funeral; perhaps there was something very final about a dark hole in the ground.

Joyce put the brake on the pram, the baby mercifully asleep, and we sisters formed a huddle, keeping our distance from the men who had been paid a pittance to shoulder our brother and were now lowering his mortal remains into the cold, damp earth. A man of the cloth stood on the other side of the trench. He was dressed in robes and a woollen scarf – I was more used to vicars in T-shirts and jeans, and this glimpse of how the wider world saw "the church" saddened me, but he had kind eyes and his were the first words we had heard spoken since walking from the safety of the car into this theatre of guilt and grief.

"We are gathered here to lay to rest Clive . . ."

We recited the Lord's Prayer – the Victorian version – in reedy self-conscious voices, and he asked us, quite gently, if we would like to sprinkle a handful of soil onto the lid of the coffin. Sarah bent to take a flower from our wreath, dropping it upon the tin plate which told his name. It had been so long since we had seen Clive, I wanted to say they must lift the lid so we might be sure it was truly him. That it wasn't all some terrible mistake. It seemed to herald our brother's final fall into an altogether different kind of darkness.

The men dispersed; I supposed they had other, more deserving bodies to manage. We nodded our thanks to the clergyman and Joyce turned the pram around to take the path back. As we left the graveside and abandoned our brother to the ground, two men appeared with shovels.

25

London, 2020

A friend who is far more organised than I, arranges an anniversary meal for those of us who trained together at Great Ormond Street in the 1970s. Ten of us gather to enjoy a lunch in London, one flying in from Alabama, and it's a joy to hear stories of what we have each done in the intervening years, professionally and personally.

When we've ordered our desserts and everyone has had an opportunity to boast about godchildren and grandchildren, I take a card from my bag. It's an oversized greetings card with a picture of pink flowers on the front and a myriad of signatures and messages inside. It's faded by time, the envelope long gone.

"Here we are," I tell my nursing friends – girls, once, from whom I learned how to grow up and be part of the teenage world during those years when we all worked and lived together. "You may not remember, but each of you signed this card back in 1975, and out of your goodness you organised a collection, though we were all penniless student nurses – £120."

Most round the table do remember, I can tell.

"It was enough to pay for a hire car to get to my brother's funeral, and flowers for his coffin."

The restaurant bill comes to a little over the equivalent amount of money today – £2,325 – and I pay it.

"I've kept the card, but I don't think I ever thanked you properly."

26

Bristol, 1966

I am eleven. The song 'Yellow Submarine' is rising through the charts and my sisters have each spent a month's wages on Beatles' handbags. Hard to save up when your earnings are taken off you every Friday night.

Joyce, at sixteen, has given up her scholarship place at The Commercial School, as did her sister before her. Now she works at C&A Modes in town as a junior shop assistant, her father taking her to the interview. After handing over most of her wage packet it leaves just enough for four days' bus fare; on the fifth day she walks.

I, too, am walking this morning, as quickly as my legs will take me, twisting through back streets of terraced housing with tiny front gardens bordered by dusty stone walls, turning this way and that in the mile and a half to Mina Road Junior School. John has run on ahead in hope of joining a game of football in the playground.

My mother is going into hospital for two days of investigations, so when I get home this afternoon she will not be there. She falls repeatedly these days, tripping up kerbs and wobbling backwards on the stairs. Now, when we go out to the grocer's or the clinic for the National Dried Milk for Sarah's baby, I must hold her hand so she is saved from stumbling into the road. It is shameful to have to walk with my mother in this way and I pray hard that I don't meet anyone from school – my fellow pupils already have enough ammunition to bully:

mismatched uniform, home-made haircuts and a father who once strode into the classroom mid-morning, mounting the platform where my teacher stood so he might more easily give him a piece of his mind.

Our parents run a greengrocery shop . . . originally, they bought and sold second-hand furniture, so we children spent our evenings polishing up table-tops or washing down dining-room chairs with vinegar water. But now our father has changed tack, and is a greengrocer and a chimney sweep. Without any kind of permission from the landlord he has removed the windows from the front of the shop, complete with wooden struts and frames. Now by day we have an open market, the ripest of Victoria plums and Cox's Orange Pippins polished to a rosy brilliance, citrus fruits from every continent cradled in tissue paper stamped with images of far-away orange groves and sun-kissed palm trees. An exotic display of extravagant abundance. And for those customers with more homely meat-and-two-veg in mind, hessian sacks of potatoes, washed clean under the kitchen tap by my mother, stand tall at the counter's edge like a row of lumpy brown soldiers.

My father has seen an opportunity in the market and has piled high, hand upon hand, green bananas for customers newly arrived from the Caribbean. Tomatoes past their best are ticketed with "Frying tomatoes, £1!", he taking a paintbrush and a bucket of whitewash to declare the special offers of the day, his beautiful script upon the one remaining window. Freshly cooked beetroot is sold by the pound, boiled up in an enamel bucket on the kitchen stove and carried, precariously, down the stairs by my mother, she up by six o'clock and ashen faced with exhaustion by opening time at nine.

We each get ourselves ready for work or school, cobbling together clean blouses, uniform and PE kits as best we can. If Clive is home from school for the holidays he must stay in bed until a shout goes up to allow him down. In this house, though no one must know, his bed is a collection of pillows and blankets in the bathroom, no sheets, where it is hard for him to rest his head against the angle of the cast-iron bath. We have a dog; an energetic border collie. We all love her in a way that has surprised us, I think; hugging her glossy black coat and enduring the frenzied licks of her tongue, rough against our faces, we have discovered an attachment which brings a joy we had not learned of before.

In the afternoons and at weekends, my father sweeps chimneys. John and I are sent out each evening after school to post leaflets through letterboxes, printed on slips of paper with a "John Bull" printing outfit to advertise the "Brush Vacuum Chimney Sweep". On Saturday afternoons and school holidays we go with him, in turn, to help carry the brushes. I have learned the trick of only turning the rods clockwise as we push them up the chimney so the brush does not unscrew itself. When I am sent out to confirm the brush has appeared out the top of the chimney pot to prove the job done well, I am schooled to say "yes" even when it can't be seen.

The greengrocery business is wildly successful, twelve people serving customers on a Saturday, the queue out the door and round the corner. Even so, there are constant arguments about the rent money so I can't be sure we will be staying here very much longer. That's how we always know we will be moving on . . . when the arguments become more heated.

My mother has left him several times, though on the last occasion only managing to get as far as spending the night in our father's van parked round the corner away from the footfall of the main road since it has no road tax. Her words as she slammed the door behind her were a brave rebellion, but in truth we all knew her shaky legs would carry her no further than the side street round the back.

On a Tuesday night in May, there is a row – the loud, vicious kind that we know will plummet the house into a deep silence for some days, so that as we walk from school John and I will need to wonder, "Will they be speaking when we get home?"

"Let's not step on the cracks in the pavement," my little brother suggests on days like these, "so we can be sure it will be alright."

The familiar threat of who-knows-what-might-happen hangs over us as we leave the kitchen to sort ourselves for bed. The row has begun as always – the housekeeping has been taken from the mantelpiece and wasted at the bookies. The landlord has called for his rent and we are six weeks behind. There is no money for the electricity meter and the dog has become a nuisance. It trips her up. She's lively and needs more walks. He should be the one to take the dog out and cook her food. It's enough to walk up and down the stairs to the shop – he goes out every evening and doesn't see what she has to put up with.

We cower under blankets so we cannot hear the shape of the words they hurl at one another, needing not to know whether she has taken her coat and gone once again. And because we cannot make out the rise and fall of the argument, we can keep believing what he tells us: that it is she who causes the upsets; that he is right and she is wrong.

The letter that comes in the morning, telling my parents of her admission to hospital for investigations, seems to distract temporarily from the mutual anger.

My teacher at Mina Road school, Mr Price, is a tall, gangly man of early middle age, always neat and tidy in a pale-grey suit, white shirt, narrow tie and highly polished black shoes. He stoops slightly, embarrassed by his height perhaps, and wears rimless spectacles with thick lenses so his watery blue eyes appear larger and more piercing than they really are. Sometimes, momentarily, he takes the spectacles off to polish them on a freshly laundered cotton handkerchief, and then he squints and blinks as though he is half blind without them. He doesn't smile often and has a cut-glass accent and an acerbic turn of phrase, but I believe he admires my spelling and neat handwriting, my father lately insisting I mimic his own, standing over me whilst I practise flourishes and loops to his satisfaction.

Often Mr Price chooses me to answer class questions, my hand shooting up quickly and confidently. I love school. I have two friends: Janet, whose birthday is six days before mine, and Mary who, like me, is predicted to do well in the exams.

This morning I arrive in a rush, clutching my satchel in my arms since it was bought second hand and is wearing thin at the corners, the plastic strap unreliable. Nevertheless, I am grateful for it. Though it is canvas rather than leather, it helps in the illusion of my being just the same as everyone else.

I am late in, the playground already deserted – it happens often, but still there is a sick feeling in my throat as I push through the green doors and half run to the classroom, my head pounding with the rush and hurry and no breakfast.

No, Mr Price, I cannot explain any more clearly why my homework has not been handed in on time, and my project on volcanoes isn't finished. Yes, I have forgotten, again, to bring in the money for the school trip.

I have constructed a story which I believed, as I half ran to school, was plausible and possible. Before I'd reached the school gates I was sure it would get me through. I cannot tell my teacher I'd cooked dinner for my family last night, because the row had made it necessary that we all should scramble to do anything we thought might turn the tide of acrimony. Or that I'd helped my mother, worn out with the effort of shouting, onto the toilet and into bed, ironed a shirt for my father to wear to the hospital and packed her a soap bag, though a decent flannel could not be found so we cut the end from an old towel.

That there was no bread or milk in the house for breakfast, and my little brother got a clip round the ear from his father for answering back so we'd left the house in a hurry without my homework folder. I could not possibly have asked for money. And when I arrive home this afternoon I must run to the corner shop, as my mother will be in hospital and there needs to be a dinner on the table for my father. He eats meat every day while we do not.

Mr Price is disappointed in me. He sees me flush with the deception, hears my floundering excuses, is perhaps extra vigilant today because it is the morning of the 11-Plus examination and he has high hopes of success for his class.

He orders me to the headmistress's office. For telling lies. I stow the satchel beneath my desk, classmates watching in some amusement as

I leave, baying for blood which is not theirs. Janet lowers her eyes to the floor as I pass.

I sit for long minutes outside the office door on a green cloth chair in the semi-darkness of a tiled corridor. "Miss Clarke", it says upon a brass plate. The door opens and I am summoned in. She is tall and stately and has no patience with liars. My mouth is clamped shut and I cannot look into her face. I must not give away the secret of what happens behind closed doors, pretence my only strategy; it protects me from falling into a shameful and unthinkable abyss.

When I return to the classroom, I am in time to sit with my peers and turn the paper to page one. I dip my pen into the inkwell and put humiliation behind me, though my hands are trembling and my heart thumping because, in truth, this is where I see the possibility of escape.

I write my name in careful cursive script at the top of the page. The examiners are people who will never meet the real me – they will never learn I am an outsider, trying my very hardest to be ordinary. They won't guess I am actually a spectator, and never have been worthy of becoming a participator.

The house is quiet when I walk in; I see the shop is locked up and remember it is half-day closing. My sisters won't be in from work for an hour or two. John is out in the backyard kicking a football against the wall; he doesn't talk to me as I pass and I wonder what kind of reception his father gave him, because I already know he has broken his third pair of glasses in a month. The boys at school are not kind to a "four eyes" in the playground.

I go upstairs intending to peel potatoes for tea, to find my father sitting at the table by the window smoking a cigarette, the evening newspaper open to the sports pages.

"Your mother won't be home for a couple of days," he tells me without looking up, hardly giving me a moment to get myself sorted at the sink. "She's had a lumbar puncture. It's multiple sclerosis; there's nothing to be done. They say she'll be in a wheelchair in a year or two."

When Sarah and Joyce come in from work we finish tea and stand at the sink together to do the dishes. Sarah washes as it's her turn, Joyce and I dry and put away. I tell them what our father has said.

"It's their Silver Wedding Anniversary today," Sarah says, not looking up from the bowl of tepid water as though it doesn't matter a bit that our mother is lying in a hospital bed and our father is down the dog track. "Let's go in tomorrow and all take her a card."

There are two scholarships awarded and I am given one, passing the 11-Plus with a distinction. I am so proud. Mr Price is proud. In fact, even my father is proud – just for a week or two, boasting to all that will listen. But in the event, I only attend the premier girls' grammar school in Bristol for a term because in the January he shuts up shop and we move to the country; at Easter we move on again, the job not to his liking. During the summer holidays, we move back to Bristol.

Three schools in my first year of secondary school, by which time no one in the world is interested that I was once a scholar.

27

Bristol, 2020

My sisters and I have made arrangements to meet for tea after my trip to the St Paul's district; this is our last opportunity to be together until after the craziness of the summer holidays. It's less than a year now, until the centenary of Mabel's birth, and I feel the pressure of nothing being sorted. Nothing thought through.

It's not the enormity of the task that bothers me. I am an amateur caterer who is never rocked by large numbers. But this business of inviting an entire village, and bringing a sense of celebration after all we've relived and discovered – this is the challenge.

I've not lingered in the street where our father's shop became such a success – the blessing of it was never enjoyed, so intent was he on doing as he pleased with the takings. I had planned to take the walk to school, but in the event it was enough to imagine it . . . I redeemed the day a little by driving through the back streets to the library, a beautiful Victorian building where, long ago, I discovered the worlds of Nevil Shute, Jane Austen and Thomas Hardy, eight books allowed each week on my cardboard ticket.

We are at the gastro-pub a stone's throw from Joyce's house. It's a cavernous space, and today there is a scarcity of customers apart from two or three tables occupied near the window, muted lighting more suited to evening trade so it's not a particularly lively place to spend an hour before I travel home.

While Joyce orders at the counter, Sarah shows me a photograph of her new puppy. It has become a full-time job, and we talk together about the mixed blessings of having dogs – the walking, the training, the mopping up, the trips to the vet.

Joyce joins us at the table; she's had a conversation with the lady on the till and it's a lovely thing to witness. "Oh my gosh!" She places cups around the table and takes a spoon to stir the tea in the pot. "It's so lovely we can have dogs of our own, now, isn't it? We loved Gyppee at that house. She was a nervy little thing but she was always so happy to see us come home! Do you remember we used to call it her funny five minutes, tearing up and down the stairs with excitement!"

"That got taken away from us, too," Sarah reminds us, "like everything else we tried to love. He took her down the dogs' home and had her put to sleep while we were all out the house."

I am growing tired of trying to find a story of Happy Endings. There has been no spark of goodness in any of our travels through childhood to lift our spirits and share moments of delight, every memory blighted by sadness. An intention to revisit misery is not how this storytelling started out.

I pour the tea. "I remember our mother being jealous of her, though – grumbling how the dog kept tripping her up. It might have been her who made him do it."

"No, she loved that dog," contradicts Sarah, hands clasped around her cup, not looking up; always the sister with the last word on truth because she was the oldest and remembers more. "He did it out of spite. She just got the blame for it."

"That house was an awful place – all those stairs, and on her feet all day in that shop!" Joyce keeps her voice light but I can see she is imagining the steep and dingy staircase between shop and flat, uncarpeted, the hotchpotch of furniture gleaned from the era of the second-hand shop, our mother struggling to count change for customers with hands that trembled, locking up at last to climb the stairs on all fours and endeavour to peel a potato.

"Him trying one thing after another, never satisfied, off down the dog track with the rent money. Do you remember that night we sneaked out to find her – after that row when she walked out?" Joyce turns to Sarah because I'm not a part of this memory. "We saw her sitting in the dark in his van round the corner – do you remember? Just the shape of her, through the windscreen."

Sarah nods, grimacing. "We didn't speak to her. I suppose we were frightened of him finding out we'd gone. We just went home again and left her there."

There are two ladies in conversation at the next table. One is talking at the other, her companion sitting with her back to us, nodding agreement from time to time though I can guess from her demeanour that she is tired of the diatribe. Apparently, a nearest and dearest has died and a hornets' nest of indiscretions has come to light. There is fury in the storyteller's voice. Even so, the listener, a lady of older years with a tight silver perm wearing an olive-green polyester jumper, is finding our conversation far more engaging than the drama described by her companion, because now she takes her elbows from the table and leans back in her chair, all the better to hear us.

And I wish that Joyce would either lower her voice or stop sharing her memories of what she saw and heard that morning our mother came home from the night in the van, things I remember nothing of because my heart has decided not to know. And this nosy eavesdropper is certain to hear the words "rape" and "slap" and "cruelty" and she will not understand that these are things of long ago and they cannot be corrected now – only resurrected to haunt us.

The teapot is drained dry, so thankfully we can go. The woman turns to watch as we pass, looking us up and down as though she has every right to judge. An undeserved shame runs like a thread through the story of my mother's life, and we are still not free.

When we began, this fairy tale was a thing of fascination and admiration; a tribute to a woman who longed to become more; a story of courage and brave adventuring. Now I've learned too much truth to want to put the words in black and white upon a page so others might be entertained.

I know I cannot write what I cannot bear to read. It's just a question of when I tell my sisters.

28

Dorset, 2020

I'm at the beach hut – by myself, just for the afternoon. A bright and sunny day, a blustery wind blows from the east and although the beach beyond my front door is busy with children and families, the grown ups are in sweatshirts, the children at the shoreline in wetsuits.

Two little girls of maybe five or six are practising cartwheels upon the sand dune at the bottom of my steps. A dog of mixed heritage runs wild and free, ears flapping in the wind, tongue lolling, a picture of bounding joy. A house sparrow alights upon a frond of marram grass, swayed this way and that by an onshore breeze. Black-headed gulls wheel and screech, sharing the same flight path as the wind takes them where it will.

I wonder, if my mother could be here with me today, what we might be doing. She would have been almost a hundred years old by now, so I can put aside the "What ifs" or "If onlys", because very probably she would already have been lost to us.

During these months of travelling through Mabel's life I've learned of her favourite songs, her favourite blouse, her dislike of things that creep and crawl, her fear of water. I know of her skill at badminton, a net rigged up across an attic room in a Bedfordshire townhouse played in secret with conspiring daughters, and her love of Radio Luxembourg, starting up at 7 p.m. by which time all chores must be finished so she might be free to sit awhile and sing along. I have learned of her deftness with a darning needle and her cleverness with an egg custard tart, steamed suet dumplings – "doughboys" – light as a feather, shortcrust pastry, sugary sweet, rubbed in by hand and baked golden. I can imagine the way she hung washing upon a line, socks two by two, shirts starched crisp and cotton sheets set free to billow in a brisk spring breeze. Terry towelling nappies boiled and bleached to a snowy white, three clothes pegs to a pair, a conjoined row of laundered perfection.

She would not, if she were here, be swimming in the sea as the lady in the nearby hut does each morning, for, as she often told us, water is dangerous. "It draws you in." And neither would she be stretched out upon a sun bed to bask in the warmth of the day – no, not even on a day set aside so we might spend it together. For it is surely a wickedness to be idle; best we work our fingers to the bone until the day we drop, since life was never meant to be enjoyed. Rather, it is our duty to be busy the whole day long.

She might, I think, tune the radio to a music station so we listen to the latest songs and hum along to the melody. She would know all the words. I would offer her tea, and she would say, "Oh, yes! That would be lovely! One-and-a-bit sugars, please." Two chairs would be set upon the porch, and as she settled – near enough to enjoy watching the sea but far enough away to be safe – the kettle would sing upon the hob as I arrange china cups and saucers on a pretty tray. The rhythm of an incoming tide at the Dorset shoreline would meld into the gentle notes of a Perry Como ballad, the radio turned down low so we might not be a nuisance to others and be shamed.

She would take her work bag upon her lap and begin again on the cable-knit cricket jumper for a favourite son, wool spun from sheep on a Scottish hillside, the skein earlier held aloft by a helpful daughter, hands set a shoulder width apart and tipped from side to side so she might wind and wind the creamy thread into a weighty ball.

She settles back into the chair, the cable needle put ready; her needles click and pause and click again, her hands quick and dexterous, her concentration complete. She is not slow, and shaking, and drooling. She is not ill.

I set the cup and saucer down upon the table at her side. A chocolate biscuit on a fluted plate.

"Thank you," she says, glancing up from her work for a moment so our eyes meet, and she smiles. And I am reminded how very pretty she is.

She sees me, and I see her. And we are known to one another, here in this place of loveliness.

Now, alone, I take a mug of tea and place it on the table where it stands across the door, open to the sights and sounds of sand and sea. I have brought my knitting – a sparkly pink jumper that only needs the finishing of a front band to be complete. I am knitting with a pair of Mabel's needles. It is a work of love for her great-granddaughter.

29

Hampshire, 2020

The plan to finish the journey through our mother's life and the homes we lived in as children has been interrupted by one of my husband's crazy schemes to gather people.

"Because we can. Simply that!" he says.

It is to be a get-together of a hundred and fifty friends and family, young and old alike, at a glorious hotel on the south coast of England. He has taken all the rooms plus an overflow to a local hotel on the river. Guests are forbidden to tell me anything about the arrangements.

I absolutely hate surprises. I am a thinker-through of all things, married to someone who loves risk and setting the scene for last-minute amazement. Bruised by being dragged from place to place to place at the whim of an irresponsible father, my security now is in meticulous pre-planning and a clear understanding of all that lies ahead.

My daughter advises me what to pack.

"You'll love it, Mum," she assures me, rummaging through my wardrobe and plucking out two dresses and a smart jacket. "The children are all really excited. Book a hair appointment."

I go along with the deception, aware that all those who know me well enough will feel a dreadful guilt at the subterfuge. And, of course, it's a wonderful event when it happens; friends from my nursing days, friends from college, friends from the business world. Young people who used to be in our church youth group and spent most of their teenage years in my house eating my food. Now they bring their own little families and it's a glorious melding of the generations.

And my cousins have come, our Auntie Jane's two daughters and Auntie Frances's eldest. Her younger sister has multiple sclerosis – a curse on three generations of Howe women, blessedly stopping short of us. We are just left with the trauma of early babies and a creeping blindness.

Sarah, Joyce and I sit with our three cousins on a cluster of chairs and sofas in the hotel lounge, a tray of tea and biscuits before us organised by my husband. We swap pictures of our grandchildren and reminisce about our mothers, those three sisters from Blagdon whose futures unfolded so very, very differently. But here we all are, their daughters now with daughters of their own, drinking tea together and spending an hour in the past.

All around us are other groups, other families; newly acquainted, contented guests certain of their place in this eclectic mix of then and now, chattering and laughing together while I am thrown back into being the person I once was. I wonder what they see, these cousins, when they look at me now.

"Cath's writing a book!" Sarah tells them, as though I am not sitting right there beside her. "About Mabel's life!" she continues, no doubt in her mind that I will actually manage it; it is simply a matter of time.

"And life in Blagdon," adds Joyce, "and how their lives changed when their mother died."

"We're visiting the places we lived, and thinking about how it was for her – to keep moving around, and never have a place to settle," explains Sarah, as though it has carried no emotional price tag to drag ourselves through the journey that was our childhood.

Frances's daughter Margaret sits back in her armchair, hands wrapped around a cup of tea, at ease with us though we meet with her at most once a year. "There's not much I can help you with there," she says. "I didn't see very much of you all when we were growing up, and as for their life in Blagdon, Mother was sent to live with that auntie in Wales as soon as Laura arrived – she always called it the time of fleas and famine!"

"Oh that's so sad!" I say without stopping to think, because I am the cousin who has lately been recording the details of those little sisters' motherless days and now the daughters of Lily Howe are real people to me. "Frances was a refugee, then, before ever the word was thought of!"

Margaret nods, her thoughts far away, I think. "She went back much later . . . to Blagdon. But she never warmed to Laura."

"Send me any photos – of the sisters," I tell her. "We only have one of Mabel in Blagdon, sitting on the steps of Glebe House with Laura and Harry and someone we think was a lodger. And two photographs of her in the garden when we were little. Everything else was lost in all the moving around."

"I've got a similar one I think, of them on the steps of Glebe House; Harry has his arm around Laura." Margaret is imagining it in her head. "She's leaning back into his arms and he seems very happy. I'll send it. Laura looks very young."

"Ours isn't like that at all!" says Sarah a trifle crossly, perhaps because none of us are ready to hear anything good about Mabel's stepmother.

"Well we were never surprised to hear you'd moved on again!" Auntie Jane's daughter says, philosophically, reaching to top up her tea from the large silver pot set between us. I notice her hands and the way she holds her cup and it reminds me of her mother and it's a lovely moment of remembrance. "Your dad certainly didn't give Auntie Mabel a chance to settle anywhere!"

I see it all – the judgements made about the latest goings-on in our household, the conversations about our feckless father, the ridiculing of the latest hare-brained scheme. These cousins who we admired, who lived in the same house their entire childhood, who joined the local Girl Guides and each week wore the proper uniform, neatly pressed by their mother and hung in a wardrobe; these girls who went on Sunday School outings and holidays to the seaside and brought friends home to tea. They could never, I think, imagine the humiliation of bailiffs at the door, the frenzy of packing life into tea chests before the landlord came to call. Or the piling of small children into the back of a van so their mother might reach the next place before dark, because there probably would be no electric turned on, and potted fish paste on dry bread for tea, the first night sleeping on bare mattresses set upon dusty floorboards with overcoats for warmth. These girls, lovely as they are, have never felt fear as we did, hiding beneath the blankets in the dark, hands over ears so we might not hear the words hurled at one parent by another, doors slamming, then listening in the blackness so we might know if our mother has left or not.

I wonder if my sisters are thinking the very same thing. Sarah is looking down into her teacup. It's yet another of those conversations about the past that may not leave my sisters in a good place and I wonder, again, if my instinct has been correct – that the continuous delving into all things long-ago is less than wise and we should call a halt to it.

"Any photos we did have of our mother got left behind," Joyce speaks into the gap between one cousin's unspoken life story and another, "because we always moved on in such a rush. I always wondered we had anything left to unpack, come the end!" Her words are said lightly; she bears no grudges.

"Oh well," Sarah's voice is loaded with cynicism, "she didn't bother to unpack the boxes after so many years of it, just left them stacked up in a passageway."

"I held onto my favourite dolls!" I am hoping to lighten the conversation because I do not want to emphasise the gulf between these daughters of favoured aunties and ourselves, the poor relations. "One with golden hair and the other silver, in green dresses with a sparkly thread and white Mary-Jane shoes." I can see them in my head, feel the weight of their plastic bodies, limbs unbending and painted faces forever smiling; I can smell the fragrance of their precious newness. I turn to my eldest cousin, "I named them after you and your sister, 'Margaret and Elizabeth', though I'd never met you! You were the one with golden hair!"

In that moment, as I look her full in the face and bring to mind the awe in which we held the daughters of a glamorous mother and an airman, I see the truth of how very far Mabel fell; the depth of derision in which her family must have held her.

Margaret has tears in her eyes as she replies, quietly, "How very special, that you would do that." And I feel there has been a meeting of minds, because she sees.

Our cousin – as down to earth as her mother, our lovely Auntie Jane, leans forward to help herself to another biscuit. "Well, we all saw how difficult Auntie Mabel's life was," her tone is matter-of-fact, "and Mother was always sure to write to Mabe every other week so she knew she was being thought about."

Her older sister nods, pushing her specs further up her nose with her knuckles – just as my Auntie Jane used to do. Her face is suddenly serious. "We all saw your dad's cruelty . . . not just to your mum but to Clive. It wasn't right, but what could anyone do?" she finishes sagely, draining her teacup and setting it back on the tray between us. "That's how things were back then."

"Well our dad spoke out good and loud that day!" continues our cousin. "When you'd all been given Sunday tea in the best room and been chatting for an hour or two before Uncle Frank got up and told you it was time to go, because young Clive was still sitting in the van outside!" Her voice is strident with remembered rage. "And there that poor blind boy was, in the van all that time! And it was cold and dark by now!"

"Oh my goodness. I'd never seen Father so angry!" Her sister closes her eyes for a second or two, whether reliving the moment or in dread of remembering it, I cannot tell. "He got right up out of his chair and shouted to Uncle Frank . . . 'Don't you ever come here again and leave that poor boy outside!' Your mother got up to go and fell right over, right there in front of everyone, and your father just stepped over her and went for the door. Our mum helped pick her up."

It's too awful to picture and I look at my sisters' faces and know I must bring us back to where we are, drinking tea in our very best dresses, watching young families play croquet on the lawn beyond the picture window; hearing the rise and fall of friendly chatter all around us muffled into a gentle rhythmic hum by the pale-grey pile of a plush hotel carpet.

I'm running out of ways to wipe awfulness from our imaginations. None of us wants to picture our mother struggling to get up from the floor in her favourite sister's parlour, all decorum lost no matter that she had worked so very hard to keep her tongue from slurred speech and her trembling hands from slopping tea into the saucer. Because here, no forgiveness is possible. I know we children would, in that moment, have sided with the loudest voice and walked obediently out to the van, leaving our mother behind to fend for herself.

Joyce cuts in. "We're thinking of organising a tea party. Well, Cath is, really! In Blagdon Village Hall. I hope you can all come? It's to celebrate the anniversary of Mabel's hundredth birthday. Exactly on the day, the twenty-fifth of July next year."

The cousins are thrilled. The mood lightens. They all agree it's a lovely idea.

"We are hoping all the village will come," explains Sarah, more animated now we have escaped from 1967. "Lots of the women who went to school with our mothers are still around. And the new people living at Glebe House are anxious to come! Shirley told me." Sarah is warming to the subject and, it seems, overanxious to emphasise the significance of the gathering. "Our mother loved that house. She often spoke about it and every time we visit Blagdon now, we always walk past and imagine her there."

I look across the width of a polished mahogany coffee table and see their faces, changed from secret shame to the anticipation of good, hear the lively excitement in their voices and feel the responsibility of making it all happen, just as they imagine. A tea party at which Mabel Howe will be celebrated, not shamed. I see it is, indeed, in danger of needing to become a certainty.

"Oh, she really did!" I hear Joyce say, wistfully. "Love Glebe House, I mean. That house was like a legend in our family. She talked about it all the time to us. It was her favourite place in all the world!"

"Well, I don't know why," our cousin says tersely, sitting up tall and straight in her chair and setting her teacup down with a loud clunk so it rattles the teaspoon. "Our mother told us the truth about what life was like for Auntie Mabel in that house!"

30

Somerset

I've travelled to Blagdon alone. It's a pilgrimage I need to make without the interruption of words. I've emailed ahead of time; the owners of Glebe House are expecting me, showing great kindness when really there's no need to indulge a complete stranger in the odd request to visit their garden.

"No, truthfully," I assured them, "it's kind of you to offer to show me the house, but I would be so grateful just to walk through to the garden, and sit there awhile."

I've chosen to come in mid-October, while the memory of my cousin's words is still fresh in my mind. I've been sure to choose a day when the autumn sun is bright, the air crisp and clear. A cheerful day in the heavenlies.

They are considerate of my request to spend time in the garden. The lady of the house brings me out a mug of tea, exchanges a few pleasantries regarding the journey down, the health of my sisters, the loveliness of autumn, and then she is gone. The garden is held in a stillness that comes when birds have forgotten how to sing and cows have been herded into their winter quarters. Lambs are long gone.

There is no shed here now, so I must guess where it might once have stood. Three raised beds of winter vegetables are neatly labelled and freshly weeded. A gravel path is edged with ornamental bricks and a bird table with a pitched roof is strung about with nets of peanuts and fat balls. A robin flutters in, takes fright and skips away.

The earthenware mug is comfortingly warm, a simple blessing on a chilly day. Beyond the hedge are wide-open fields, brown unploughed earth left fallow now until spring comes upon the village. Far away and to the left, a coppice of trees is heavy with sheltering rooks. They rise and fly as one, then settle once again, their cries muffled by the distance between us. To the right I can just make out the trees which border Garston Lane, where young Mabel Howe's story began.

I wonder, did she creep along this garden path the night she fled, or did she run? Was she ready and willing to leave all she'd ever known to give herself to a dreamer, a story-teller? Or was it merely the recklessness of a moment, encouraged by a young man who saw the fragility, the longing of her heart to belong?

I think about the photo which hangs upon my wall in Buckinghamshire. A sepia photograph of a handsome young man, kept through all the years of leaving, of moving from place to place to place. I gave a copy of it to each of my sisters, and my younger brother John. When my back was turned, so my sisters tell me, he smashed it to the floor, hurling the jagged pieces of glass into the bin.

But the photograph that was Mabel's own – the original "From your Frankie" inscribed on the back – remains. Perhaps, after all, she loved him enough to keep it safe.

I text my sisters as soon as I get back to the car. No need to explain I've visited Blagdon without them – they will assume that is something I would never do. Better they think I've sorted everything by email.

"I've booked the Village Club," I tell them, "for Mabel's birthday, next year."

"How exciting!" Sarah is, predictably, thrilled. "It's going to be such a wonderful day! How many people will it hold, did they say?"

Joyce is of a more practical nature. "Did you ask how many chairs they've got?"

"Shall we all go next week and take a look around? See Shirley again? She will have lots of ideas! I'll email her now," Sarah responds, helpfully.

Joyce texts back: "Where are you now? I thought you were going to Dorset?"

I send a brief reply to both, not explaining where I am or the anxiety of the day to come. "She's going in tomorrow for the baby to be induced."

I don't need to say more because they've shared the grief of two granddaughters born too early and lost in a matter of moments.

"Keep in touch," says Sarah.

"Send our love, won't you," says Joyce.

Dorset happens. Though the weather is unpredictable, my husband and I go anyway. We open the double doors and latch them back to watch the ebb of the tide.

"Best we don't keep reminding ourselves about how much we paid," he says, wrapped up warm in a quilted jacket and woollen scarf, "because it was worth it. But you know we did, don't you? Overpay, I mean."

We did; we certainly did. And it's possibly a shameful thing when I consider my mother Mabel, sleeping in a shed in her stepmother's garden while a rat scurried and scratched in the corner.

I fill the kettle from the standpipe outside and set it on the gas cooker. The flick of a switch and it's on. I hope Mabel would be pleased to see the simple pleasure of it. To be thrilled that her youngest daughter, who never knew her to be well, has reinvented the story of her life, recounting a deeper truth of who she was and who she strived so hard to become.

My husband and I sit together on our little wooden balcony in the fading light of early evening to watch the coming and going of the sea; a quiet celebration, drinking tea in cups of blue and white china.

The history of heartache and loss has finally been put behind us. Mabel's legacy has been interrupted; a line has been drawn. My daughter has been safely delivered of a baby girl; she has named her after my mother.

PART THREE

Rhythms of a Lesser Life

1

Bristol, 1966 – 1967

On a weekend in mid-summer, a spell of gloriously warm weather cried out for a trip to the seaside. Struggling one-handedly to create some kind of order in the kitchen, the Zimmer frame a barrier between herself and the worktop, Mabel heard Frank telling the children they were all off to Weymouth the next day. A treat.

"Get yourselves up and out early," said their father as he came upstairs from a quiet Saturday in the shop he'd so recently moved them to, a stone's throw from the city centre and next to a pub, surrounded by the constant traffic of a one-way system. "We'll leave about nine. Make sure we take some sandwiches with us."

They didn't set off as early as planned. They never did. It took a while for Mabel to get herself up, lifting a leg to put her skirt on, wobbling as she attempted the putting on of underwear, giving in eventually and leaving the knickers on the floor where they'd fallen. Joyce helped with the button on her skirt and buckled the stiff leather strap on the calliper. Mabel tilted her chin as her daughter fought with the top button of her blouse.

"How did you get on with the sandwiches? Did you manage?" she asked, throat straining upwards and her mouth dry. It wouldn't do to drink too much if they were going to be in the car for hours on end.

"Yes, all done," said Joyce. "Let's leave that top button, shall we?" She reached for her mother's jumper, a turquoise affair much stained, hand-washing no match for the spilling of food. She pulled the jumper down over her mother's face, dislodging Mabel's glasses and catching her hair in the zip at the back. "I'll just go and make Daddy another cup of tea, so we can chivvy him up to get going. Sit back down on the bed a minute, have a rest before we tackle the stairs."

Three hours out of Bristol and the Austin A40 was taking the hill down into Weymouth, drifting in neutral so the radiator wouldn't boil. Mabel had dozed off from time to time in the stuffiness of the car, but the four children in the back were jostling, elbowing, restless, packed shoulder to shoulder across the seat, bare legs sticking to hot leather in the heat of the day. It seemed like it was hard for anyone to remember why this had sounded like a good idea.

Joyce had just suggested another rendition of "Ten Green Bottles" when the car swung around the arc of the hairpin bend and she cried, "I can see the sea!" and they all could except, of course, Clive, though he caught their excitement and laughed out loud, feeling the importance of the moment, swaying forward and back, all the better to be part of the anticipation of joy.

And there it was, sparkling diamonds in the sunshine far below, magical in the possibilities offered for adventure. Mabel felt her heart leap – because the seaside had always been such a special place for her, and now here they were!

Frank joined the line of cars, each packed full of day-trip paraphernalia, to park in his favourite car park, The Swannery (though she had never seen any swans), and the children flung open the doors allowing the sunshiny, salty air to cool and refresh. All tedium forgotten, in the blink of an eye the children were loading themselves up with bags of towels, buckets and spades, bottles of lemonade and grey wool blankets so heavy that shoulders slumped with the weight of it all. Clive, sensing the excitement around him and swaying ever more wildly as he held onto his little brother's arm, lifted his face to the afternoon sun and grinned at the world in general and nothing in particular.

Frank went off to pay the man in the ticket office and Mabel waited, hearing the excitement in the children's voices, their eagerness to find the beach, the teasing of one child of another. In previous years she might have helped to carry the picnic, or take Clive's arm to guide him across the car park. She could have shouldered the bag of towels, tucked John's shirt into his shorts so he might be tidied up, taken a hanky to dab at the marmalade on Clive's chin.

She used both hands to lift her heavy legs from the footwell of the car to the tarmac so she would be ready when Frank came to help.

"Hold on, Mummy," Joyce advised, coming quickly to hold the car door from closing on Mabel's legs, "Daddy's on his way back to help you out."

Frank hauled the wheelchair from the boot. "This weighs a ton," he complained under his breath, though she heard him quite clearly as he wheeled it round. He hoisted Mabel clumsily from seat to seat. Joyce slung canvas bags of sandwiches from the handles and they were off across the car park, a straggly band of old and young ready to be cautiously hopeful of an afternoon of joy.

The esplanade was a riot of noise and colour – pretty frocks of a thousand mothers, grandfathers dressed for a day out in collars and ties, little children in khaki shorts and white cotton shirts. The promenade, tarmac sizzling in the heat of early afternoon, was swarming with people of all shapes and sizes and humming with the babble of excited voices. Fathers roared at their children to "Keep up!" while others chased runaway toddlers escaping from pushchairs piled high with picnic baskets and towels, crossing Frank's path at a moment's notice as he weaved his way through with Mabel's chair. The children sidestepped grannies with oversized beach bags and boys with footballs and giant spades, John steering his older brother with a hand beneath his elbow.

Mabel sat tense and not a little afraid in the wheelchair, at the mercy of bags and buckets held carelessly from a stranger's arm or swinging freely from the handle of a pushchair. At waist height to the masses, she could do nothing but hope Frank was paying enough attention to keep her safe – she knew he would already be looking all around for a space on the sand below the wall.

She was surrounded on all sides by the sights and sounds of the seaside in summer – something which had, so many times in the past, filled her with a lightness of heart. The laughter of little children, the yapping of wayward dogs straining on leads, the chiming of the Jubilee Clock on the seafront, the tinkling melody of the ice-cream van parked conveniently near the public toilets. The people crowding her wheelchair on either side and dashing across her path were a frightening thing, a mass of careless rush and tear.

At the top of a flight of stone steps down to the sands, Frank put the brake on the chair. "Wait here, you kids. I'll go and find the lifeguards."

Families with three or four children apiece squeezed past them, so clearly had Frank left them in everyone's way. Mothers already at the end of their patience tut-tutted, pushing past the younger ones standing in quiet obedience to wait for their father. John dragged Clive out of harm's way and the boy swayed gently to and fro, a hand grasping the railings. "Can you smell the sea?" he asked his brother, a broad grin on his face as he twirled his head this way and that in excitement.

Mabel pulled her skirt down over her knees as well as she could as two young lifeguards arrived back with Frank. Blond haired and blue eyed in skimpy red shorts and tightly fitting T-shirts, they linked arms to fashion a seat and she shuffled across onto it. "We haven't done this before, Missus," the younger boy told her; Mabel guessed he might be fifteen. "Shout if we're not being careful."

They set off, walking sideways, crablike, taking the steps slowly, one at a time. Mabel felt the boys' hands beneath her bottom and remembered she was wearing no knickers. She found she was laughing, though she couldn't have said why.

Scarcely a yard or two between each family gathering, plenty of witnesses watched as the little scene played out. Frank manhandled the wheelchair down the steps after Mabel, John chaperoning Clive –

he with one hand extended to follow the contours of the wall, the other hand sweeping this way and that in wide semi-circles, fingers splayed, searching the airspace before him for hazards that might trip or catch him unawares. He was an object of curiosity, descending the concrete steps at high speed whilst looking wildly around in the wrong direction. Mabel could see the fascination on the faces of those who gawped.

He called out to his little brother behind him, "How many steps left?"

"Keep going," replied John unhelpfully and Mabel looked behind to advise – though her mouth would not speak. She saw Clive land with a jolt onto the sand as the last step took him by surprise.

The lifeguards cradled her, step by step, across the beach, their breath warm on her face. She rose and fell with their staggering progress, looking around her just enough to see the onlookers, the strangers enjoying the novelty of a free show. She dropped her head so she couldn't see their faces and they would not see hers. The little company weaved its way amongst windbreaks and sandcastles and deckchairs, eventually finding a circle of space to pitch up.

"Where do you want her, mate?" asked the boy, and Mabel opened her eyes to get her bearings and stop her head from spinning as they whirled her around to face the sea.

Frank opened up the wheelchair, fighting now against the sand as the wheels caught and stuck fast, beads of sweat on his brow. "Thank you, chaps," he signalled for them to lower Mabel into the seat, "this'll do nicely." Her skirt had ridden up to expose the whiteness of her knees; a length of petticoat showed, a glimpse of bare thigh. "I'll give you a shout when we need help to get back up," Frank said, oblivious.

The older boy nodded. "Our shift finishes at three, so it will be someone else."

"Thank you," said Mabel, though the boys had already turned to go and, anyway, the words were a mumble and she needed to wipe her chin of dribble.

The younger children unpacked buckets, spades, paper flags. There was an initial squabble about where and how the castle was to be built. Cath wanted turrets, John a deep moat. Mabel, content for a moment to watch, used her hands to hoist her legs up, one at a time, onto the foot plates of the chair, relieved to take the weight off the calliper.

Joyce came to drape a towel over her mother's knees, "So they won't burn in the sun, Mummy," she said, tugging the lumpy tweed of her mother's skirt flat beneath her. Turning her head to one side, Mabel screwed up her eyes against the glare of the sun and looked beyond where she sat so she might see the glint of the sea, but the beach was too full of deckchairs and children and people; too busy with bodies rushing here and there and shouting, calling, shrieking. And perhaps the tide was a long way out. Perhaps, after all, she had been settled too far from the water's edge.

Her head ached from the heat of the sun; she would have liked to shade her eyes, but her arm was too heavy to raise a hand. Her throat was parched. Perhaps, if Frank should offer, she would nod a "yes" to an ice lolly – so much easier than swallowing a drink. And she could taste it now, a strawberry loveliness of cool ice, softening her tongue and loosening her throat.

Frank, in a deckchair next to her, lit a cigarette and handed it to Mabel before lighting a second one for himself. "Mind you don't drop it onto your lap, now," he said. He was settled in for the day and had no thought of ice lollies. He took a pound note from his pocket and sent Cath for a tray of tea. He'd brought his paper and he retreated behind it, quite content.

"Let us know if you need anything, Mabe," he said.

Perhaps she should simply close her eyes, and stop trying. She wondered if this long, long day would ever end. The cigarette dropped from her fingers, her lips too dry to contemplate putting it to her mouth. It fell, still alight, onto the sand.

True to the BBC weather forecast, the day was hot. Relentless sunshine, and not a cloud in the sky to offer any hope of shade. Mabel felt the sweat running down her back, the green plastic of the wheelchair scorching hot. Her hair was plastered to her face; no one had thought to help her off with her jumper. The steel rod of the calliper had twisted round just enough to give a dull pain in her ankle and she knew her feet, in the brown leather lace-ups, would be swelling with the heat, she had been sitting for so long. She was thirsty, but did not dare drink. No, she wouldn't put herself through the humiliation of those boys carrying her to the lavatory. Best to try and hold on till she got home. And it was so very noisy on the beach, Mabel could feel the blood pounding in her head and her eyes ached with squinting into the glare of the sun.

There was barely an inch of sand to be seen now – and children! Hundreds of children! Half-dressed, some shockingly stark naked, and all of them shouting, screaming, arguing, running back and forth in front of where Mabel sat, flinging sand from spades and seawater from buckets. More and more day trippers had arrived to hem them in so that Clive, seated on the sand next to Frank's deckchair, had plenty of spectators. Several ladies in flowery cotton dresses, one or two in straw sunhats with "Kiss Me Quick" scrawled on bands of yellow ribbon, watched the boy with undisguised curiosity as he used his hands to dig at the pile of sand between his knees. Mabel knew this game – never with any purpose in mind, it was played simply for the pleasure of feeling the warm grains trickle through his fingers. An enjoyment all of the moment. Clive lifted his hands, the grains fell again to the sand, he scooped and lifted them again, the grains fell. He was laughing, not needing to share his game but staring up into the heavens and generally living in a world all of his own making. It was a scenario that invited others to stare. She could see their fascination, their unashamed curiosity, their condescension – as though because he couldn't see them, it didn't matter that they stared. Now and then they turned to one another to exchange a comment – a judgement, perhaps. Easy entertainment on a lazy summer afternoon.

Mabel remembered Frank's words, "He'll never be right," and wondered if, had they fought more, loved more, her son's story might have been very different. She wondered why, on summer days when she had been well, she had not taken the trouble to teach her son how to build a sandcastle.

It was way past dinner time; Joyce came back from where she'd been exploring the shops full of trinkets and bric-a-brac and unpacked the sandwiches and lemonade. Corned beef sandwiches with tomato sauce, warm from the heat of the day, wrapped in Lyon's greaseproof bread wrappers and moulded to the shape of the bag. The children gathered, their big sister spread a blanket and found plastic cups. Held in sandy fingers the sandwiches were gritty, washed down with red lemonade. A feast. Joyce thrust a cup into her blind brother's outstretched hand, adjusting his hold and reminding him to keep it straight.

"A *Famous Five* picnic!" twelve-year-old Cath said, smiling as Joyce handed round the lemonade. "Is there any cake?"

John said he didn't like fizzy, but Joyce said there was no choice, so he drank it anyway.

"Can we buy an ice cream later?" he asked his father.

Mabel knew Frank had had a good week on the horses; she heard him say "yes" and was hopeful. Chocolate bars, gooey and melted beyond recognition came from the bottom of the bag. Joyce shared them out, though Mabel shook her head, and the children licked the liquid chocolate from the wrappers, not wanting any of the treat to go to waste.

"He's going to get chocolate all over him," Frank warned as Joyce took the paper from Clive's and placed it into his hand. She ignored her father and gave it to her brother anyway.

Mabel told her daughter she wasn't hungry, already having said "no" to the sandwiches. Her throat was too dry to swallow and, anyway, there wasn't really enough food to go round. Mabel fumbled in the seat of her wheelchair for the hankie Joyce had tucked there, wiping her chin with a hand that shook. It was all too much effort. She closed her eyes against the glare and the noise and the impossibility of trying.

She must have slept through the ice-cream interval. When she woke, Frank was sending John off with the empty tea tray, calling after him, "Don't forget the deposit!" and getting up from his deckchair to tell Joyce, "Best we start packing up, the roads will be busy going back. I'll go and fetch those chaps to give us a hand." He folded his deckchair and stowed the newspaper in the nearest bag.

All around them, family groups were indeed clearing their patch of sand to go. A general exodus was happening up the steps from the beach and along the promenade.

Joyce helped Clive to his feet, brushing him down. "Stand there for a minute." She began to collect together the bits and pieces of their day. "Do you want the toilet, Mummy?"

Mabel shook her head. She dreaded those boys coming to scoop her out of the chair, because she couldn't be sure she hadn't leaked onto the seat while she slept. Cath picked up her mother's bag from the sand. She opened the zip and found Mabel a clean hanky. "Do you need to wipe your mouth, Mummy? Gosh you must be hot! Have you had that jumper on all day?"

The lifting, the jerking and bumping of being pushed along the crowded pavements back to the car park, up and down kerbs, barging through lines of families and dogs all desperate to be off home. Mabel, at waist height to the bustling and ill-tempered world around her, felt like she was being used as a battering ram. Hoisted into the car, less carefully at this end of the day, Mabel sank gratefully into the seat. Her head was thumping. The children were cranky, hot and tired, and Frank was irritated by everything: the time it took to load up bags, stowing them into the boot of the car in random disorder, the bickering of the children as they sorted who would sit by who and who could be next to the window. John was in tears, the sunburn on his shoulders red raw and beginning to blister. "I can't lean back!" he yelled at his sister, elbowing her as she endeavoured to push him further along the seat.

"Sort yourselves out!" Frank bellowed. "Clive, move yourself along! Give your brother more room!"

Mabel knew it wasn't at all fair. Nothing was fair. She closed her eyes, head lolling forward so that as Frank got in beside her he reached over and pushed her back into the seat.

"Careful, Mabe," he said. " Sit yourself back." He changed gear to accelerate, overtaking a motorbike at speed so the girl riding pillion clasped ever more tightly to her boyfriend, slim body swinging with the swerve of the bike. At long last and after much cursing under his breath, Frank turned into the stream of traffic taking the hill. "I think you should let us strap you into the seat next time we do a long journey," he told her, not unkindly, "otherwise you're going to keep bumping your head on the dashboard."

"We could try winding a scarf around your middle, Mummy," cut in Joyce from the back seat. "That would keep you safe."

Mabel closed her eyes, thrusting her shoulders back against the hot leather though it took all her strength. Her leg was twisted from the awkward bundling into the car, her knee pressing hard against the glove compartment. She must not complain; there was the journey home to contend with and the inevitable clear up from the day out. It had surely been the longest day she could ever remember. And she would need to crawl up the stairs, after all this sitting around; there was no usefulness left in her legs.

2

Bristol, 1968 – 1969

There had been too many bouts of pneumonia, too many falls, too many call-outs to the ambulance service. Frank was resistant to change – he was making a go of the paraffin and firewood business and saw no need to move, but the West Country floods of 1968 left him no choice. The house and shop were uninhabitable with floodwater damage and condemned by the authorities. Despite the history of non-payment of rent, Frank's family was to be rehoused by the council.

Mabel was secretly hopeful. There was a new freedom coming, an end to being held prisoner on the first floor. The peace and quiet of an ordinary street instead of being stranded amidst a sea of constant traffic.

Number thirty-three was set halfway along an endless ribbon of road with bland, semi-detached council housing on either side, regulation colours on front doors. Knowle seemed a forgotten backwater after the incessant busyness of Hotwells.

True to its word, the Social Work department had converted the front garden into a carport with a dropped kerb to the road, so Frank was able to swing the car onto the concrete. Once hauled from the car, Mabel needed only to be shepherded three or four steps to the house. Ground-floor doorways had been widened to accommodate her wheelchair, delivered in a furniture van hired the previous day courtesy of a grant from the Benefits Office.

"Here we are, Mummy," Joyce took her mother's arm to walk her through the hallway. "This room at the front is going to be your bedroom."

The room was not large, scarcely space enough to walk around a hospital bed with a blue plastic mattress, a chest of drawers under the window and, in the far corner and pressed up tight to the wall, a commode with a wooden seat, an enamel pan beneath. A brown luggage label on the steel tubing of the armrest announced "Bristol City Council". An uncontested surrendering to the world of the disabled.

"I don't want to go to bed yet."

"I think you need a rest after all that walking," Joyce contradicted her mother. "I'll find a sheet and make the bed up. You can have a lie down while we get on."

3

Bristol, 1969

Twelve months in, Mabel's days were orchestrated by the monotonous rhythm of being taken from here to there and back again. She knew the changing of the seasons only by the progress of a cherry tree outside her bedroom window; the fresh buds of that first early spring, the glorious canopy of midsummer when the splash of red brightened the monochrome of a concrete carport, the bleaching of colour as autumn came. A hedge, neglected enough by Frank to run wild, was mercifully forever green. The heads of passers-by bobbed up and down above the rampant privet; guessing where they were going to or coming from was an entertainment during hours of endless looking. The precinct at the end of the road, perhaps, or the pub on the corner. Little children on their way to school could, contrarily, be heard but not seen.

It was a monotony borne of necessity, because two people were needed to dress her in these days of helplessness, Cath too slight to manoeuvre her mother single-handedly between bed and commode in such a confined space.

Mabel realised this particular November day must be a Tuesday because she saw the coal truck pull up outside, heard Frank go to the door, the exchange of words, then Frank closing the door and calling to ask Cath if she was ready. They came to get her dressed, hoisting her from bed to commode, leaving her there for some time – "So we can be sure you've finished," Cath told her, Mabel's skin pinched red by the sharp edge of the pan, her back aching from the effort of sitting up.

"Come on, Mummy, let's get you off." Her bottom had suckered itself to the pan.

With some difficulty, and with the help of the Zimmer frame, Cath and Frank walked Mabel from bedroom to living room. Cath circled the scarf at her mother's waist, securing it around the back of the chair with a double knot. The pull of it dug into Mabel's ribcage as she slumped forward, but her daughter was not to know that and speech was impossible after so much exertion.

A lock of Mabel's steely grey hair fell across her face and Cath tucked it behind her ear so it might not get caught up in the food, sitting as she was to feed her mother a dish of cereal mashed to a pulp with warm milk and a generous spoonful of sugar. She placed her mother's hands around the plastic invalid cup of lukewarm tea, so she could tip it to her mouth for herself.

Mabel, wanting to oblige, drank. She preferred tea to be scalding hot but they had long ago discovered that lukewarm was safer. Her daughter seemed more animated today – more willing. She came to set Mabel's legs straight, so the calliper would not twist and rub against the bone of a bare ankle. "The social worker's calling later," she told her mother.

Mabel grunted, exhausted from the business of being hoisted from here to there and the swallowing of the cereal, spooned into her mouth whether she was hungry or not. "Can you put the television on?" came out as one long, indistinct word, but Cath understood and did as her mother asked. It was a children's programme.

"Gosh, Mummy, this used to be our favourite when John and me were little!"

Mabel could not recall. It seemed so very long since she had been surrounded by the busyness of small children. A passing memory of a country garden of vegetable patches and the clucking of chickens flitted across her mind and was gone.

The passing of the hours of this day, like every other day, was measured by cups of tepid tea, a television programme, the midday news, music on the wireless, trips to the commode. Next-door's dog had been let loose in the garden, hollering at the door all morning long. When Mabel watched the faces of Frank and Cath as they came and went from the room, they did not seem to either notice or mind. Perhaps, thought Mabel, in passing in and out of the room, the incessant barking did not disturb their thoughts in the same way it punctuated hers.

She raised a heavy hand to wipe clumsily at her chin, the handkerchief crumpled and already sodden with dribble. It might soon be time for dinner. The feeder cup had slipped from her grasp and tipped cold slops into her lap.

She had been bound to the house, this room, this chair, since she couldn't remember when. With the relentless patter of rain against the glass all night long there was no hope of an outing in the car. Or, perhaps, a visit to Jane's. For a day or two Frank had kept her company, the wind and weather too wild to contemplate the outdoors. But today, the clouds less threatening, he was driven by boredom to take his coat from the chair.

"See you later, Mabe," he said, leaving soon after the ritual of moving Mabel from one place to another.

He'd taken the newspaper, the bookies the only possible destination.

"Where's Joyce?" she slurred as her daughter came to help her sit more straight in the chair.

"At work, Mummy," Cath answered, "at the post office. Don't you remember?"

She didn't remember. Or she wouldn't have asked.

"I'm just going out to the shed for more coal," Cath told her. "We've just had a delivery. I won't be a minute."

Mabel was tired of this room. It was drab and dreary; the fireplace beside her chair piled high with cold ash was never lit before teatime. As Frank liked to remind her, they lived on benefit now – there weren't spare pound notes for luxuries. The wooden carriage clock on the mantelpiece ticked away the seconds and minutes, measuring the hours until Mabel would be moved from one room to another. There were sounds of industry coming from the kitchen, Cath taking saucepans from a cupboard, drawing water from the tap, taking a peeler, perhaps, from the drawer. Mabel imagined the weight of the pan, the slippery handle of the peeler, the splash of the water, the flare of the gas. It was all so very, very familiar, but all so very far from any hope she had of doing it herself.

Perhaps Cath might think to help her into the wheelchair, so she might be wheeled through to the kitchen for a while. This room held no cheerfulness, brown furniture set about here and there, all mismatched and second hand; a standard lamp, seldom lit, in the corner behind Frank's chair. Perhaps it had no light bulb. Brown wallpaper did nothing to reflect light from the window on a grey day in winter. The solitary window opposite Mabel's chair overlooked a back garden where dustbins and an abandoned fridge stood together next to a wooden fence. In days gone by, Mabel might have fed a friendly robin there.

The dog next door was barking more hoarsely now since he had been left out there for some hours. And in the rain. She closed her eyes, weary of looking. Her thoughts wandered; she recalled the warmth of summer days long past, of her garden at Lockleaze, flowerbeds of Sweet Williams and snapdragons, of cups of tea with a friend whose name she could not bring to mind. The joy of early morning birdsong as she pegged nappies upon a line or walked the pram to the shops, her little girls in pretty, hand-smocked dresses and white cotton socks. And Farmborough – or was it Eaton Bray? That house had brought her moments of simple pleasures, scattering corn for a hundred chickens that pecked and fussed about her feet. Or Clevedon, the salty air fresh and clean on her face as she walked the children to the playground at the beach; long midsummer evenings.

The rain persisted; there would be no trips to the seaside to watch the gentle lapping of waves upon a golden seashore, paddling with her children, dresses tucked in knickerlegs and childish skin burnt to a painful crimson. No walking of prams to a park with swings and roundabouts and miniature trains circling a green, set next to a sea wall, funnels puffing grey smoke into a blue sky. Had that been Clevedon? She made herself think. Yes, she could recall the road which led to the grassy space by the sea wall, the beach cafes that sold crisps and sugary buns baked hard through sitting on a china platter in the afternoon sun, tepid tea in thick china cups, candy floss in plastic bubbles of sticky sweetness. A cafe kitchen where she stood at the sink with a bowl of potatoes, the chatter and banter of women all around her. She closed her eyes, worn out with the longing. Because those days were then, and this was now.

"Clive's coming home soon, Mummy!" declared Cath, bringing her mother a tray with a dish and spoon. She retrieved the plastic cup, dabbing her mother's skirt with a tea towel and placing the tray across Mabel's lap, settling it straight. "Daddy's going to fetch him."

Mabel could not guess how much time had passed since she had closed her eyes to rest. She'd been imagining a beach, she knew. The shingle at Clevedon. The fragrance of a summer garden planted out by her Frankie when times were good. Had that been Lockleaze? No, Carol was there in her daydream, and she had died long before Lockleaze. Carol Ann. Blonde and blue eyed. Born too early. Delicately small, fair skin the colour of creamy milk, sitting prettily in her coach-built pram in a shell pink matinee jacket, hand-knitted, a pretty featherstitch pattern with matching bonnet and booties. Mabel imagined the pattern, from back in the day when Frances had a little job, creating matinee jackets for the front of knitting patterns. She'd posted it to her. It had surprised Mabel, that her sister had need of earning her own money. She remembered now – Frances had bought her own car.

"I'm sorry to say," Cath had read aloud from Jane's most recent letter, "that I asked Frances but she doesn't want to come with me next time I visit you. Her MS is a few years behind yours and she's frightened of seeing her future."

Cath was talking about Clive. She struggled to sit up straighter so her speech might be made more clear.

"Is school finished, then? For Clive?"

Cath took a moment to answer, tucking a tea towel around her mother's neck by way of a bib. "He's been in Surrey," the girl replied in a patient tone, as though she were talking to a small child. "At a training centre. You remember. He can't stay – his fits are too much of a problem. He's put a length of cane through his wrist in the basket-making workshop."

She'd not thought – of course, he must be past his teens by now. She must be stupid, not to remember.

Cath brought a dish of lukewarm tomato soup and sat beside Mabel to spoon it into her mouth. "Clive will be company for you," she said.

They persevered with the soup but much of it dribbled from the sides of her mouth. Mabel shook her head between one spoonful and another, exhausted from the effort. "No," she said, thickly, attempting to wipe her chin with a hanky. "No more."

"Okay, Mummy, I'll clear up. You can have something later if you're hungry. Do you need the commode?" She took the tea towel from around Mabel's neck.

Mabel shook her head again. It was too much trouble. She would hold on. She sat for a while, looking straight ahead at nothing in particular, hearing Cath clattering dishes and cutlery at the sink in the kitchen, raindrops pattering steadily against the window opposite her chair; rivulets of water sketching patterns of glistening silver.

She wondered if Frank would be back soon. And Clive was coming home! He loved the wireless. She loved the wireless, though Cath often forgot to put it on for her. She and Clive would listen together. To the cricket, perhaps – Clive loved the cricket. She believed he knew every score from every Test Match since the war. But no, now she came to think more clearly, it wasn't summer any longer. Winter had come.

Mabel was aware of her daughter moving about the room; the repositioning of a chair, the tidying of newspapers upon a table. Cath began to lay the fire in readiness to put a match to it once evening came upon them. She arranged kindling, a few sticks, nubs of coal tipped from a shovel. "Would you like a cup of tea, Mummy?"

"Can you put the wireless on?" she asked her daughter. "Music. It would be nice to have some music." She couldn't be sure the words had come out right. Sometimes Cath brought her a pencil and a pad of paper to try and write something down, but spidery letters scrawled across a page were hard to decipher and after an awkward silence, Cath often took the paper and pen away and changed the subject.

The girl came to wipe her mother's chin. "I'll bring the commode through. It'll be quicker than walking you back and you haven't been on it for ages."

Mabel was sure the child didn't mean to be cruel, but really – all she wanted was to close her eyes and listen to something lovely. Just to rest.

Mabel heard the squeaking of the wheels as her daughter brought the cumbersome thing from the front room to set it directly beside her. Cath untied the scarf that held Mabel in the chair and leant forward to hoist her up onto her feet, twisting her round to sit squarely on the cold rim of the pan. Mabel wore no underwear – it had become too much for Cath to dress her mother in knickers and slips and it was many months since Mabel's body had needed a bra. She sat, every ounce of strength needed to stop herself from falling forwards, wondering if Frank would soon be home and she might see Clive.

"I've finished," she told her daughter, her voice hoarse and cracked, words slurred, but when she looked around Cath had gone upstairs on some kind of errand, so she must wait a little longer for help.

4

Bristol, 1969

A wild and windy October tipped into a wet and murky November, summer a distant memory. On waking to another grey dawn, Cath saw the raindrops hurling themselves horizontally at the uncurtained bedroom window and knew the day ahead would be a dreary one. No chance of pushing her mother's wheelchair into the back garden for ten minutes while she pegged out the washing, or sitting on the front doorstep with a cup of tea to watch the world go by while Mabel dozed after breakfast was done.

In the bed next to her Joyce fidgeted and then sighed – reluctant, perhaps, to step out onto the stone-cold Lino.

"Morning," Cath said, quietly. "I'll get dressed and go and make you a cup of tea."

Their father could be heard coughing and spluttering as he came upstairs to use the toilet. His chest was always bad first thing in the morning.

"What day is it?" Joyce mumbled, blanket half covering her face.

"Um . . . Wednesday I think. No, Tuesday." Hard for her to know. Every day was just the same as the one that came before and the one that came after. She needed to stir herself; John must be got from his bed or he would miss the bus to school. "Get a move on, or you'll be late for work," she told her sister.

"I need your car today," said their father as Joyce came down the stairs. "I'm fetching Clive after dinner."

Joyce didn't answer but Cath saw her face; if he had told her yesterday she could have got to work on time. Now, with two different buses to catch, she would be late. Her sister took a coat from the bannister and left without saying goodbye, slamming the door with some force.

"I'll help you get your mother up," Frank told Cath. "I'm off out later."

He picked up last night's paper from the chair by the fireplace and sat, opening it to the racing results. "Get me another cup of tea when you're ready."

"You'll miss the social worker." She cleared cups and plates from the table. "He's calling in about two, he said."

"These people just do what they have to," Frank settled himself behind the paper. "Don't expect any help from them!"

Oh but she did! Because today, Cath remembered as she put the kettle on to boil water ready for the washing-up, he had promised to bring her a typewriter!

It was the usual struggle that exhausted them all in equal measure. Hoisting her mother from bed to commode, Cath tugged the nightie over Mabel's head and replaced it, one heavy arm at a time, with a vest. Then a jumper. She brought her mother a cup of tea in a plastic cup with a spout, because the longer she could persuade her to sit on the commode the better. It saved a trip back to the bedroom later. When Mabel said she'd finished, Frank came through to haul her to her feet so Cath could manoeuvre a skirt over one foot and then the other, buttoning it at the waist. Then the calliper, strapped as tight as it would go so the steel rod stayed straight and wouldn't twist as Mabel walked. Last of all the brown lace-up shoes. No stockings; they had long since abandoned underwear.

"Let's get you in your chair then, Mabe." Frank brought the Zimmer frame, and then began the slow, slow three-person shuffle round the end of the bed, along the passage and across to her chair by the fireplace. They were all relieved to be done, Mabel's head jolting back as she half-fell into the chair, her breathing laboured.

Cath bent to straighten her mother's legs and tug her skirt so it was flat beneath her bottom.

"Let me strap you in, Mummy, and then I'll get your breakfast."

After the exertion of swallowing down the cereal, the wireless went on and Mabel was content to be left. Her head lolled forward and she dozed.

Cath was glad of an hour or two to tidy up – the doors between the downstairs rooms had been removed by the council so there was nowhere to hide any muddles from visitors. Then lunch time – a bowl of soup for her mother, a biscuit for herself. The commode was an ever-present chore. She swilled it out with disinfectant and tipped the contents down the drain outside the back door.

The social worker was late, which was a good thing, and when he finally arrived he was apologetic and flustered. A tall, lanky man, he wore horn-rimmed black spectacles and, as always, a tartan scarf twisted around his neck. Never a coat, so today there were speckles of rain across the shoulders of his suit jacket. His little-boy haircut and the glasses combined gave him the look of someone who was too young for the job.

Frank had commented more than once that he was most probably new to it – unqualified, since there was little anyone could offer the family in the way of help. "They're just checking up on us to see if we're still entitled to benefit," was his opinion.

Cath, answering the knock at the door, opened it wide.

"Here you are," he said, "I didn't forget." He scuffed his feet upon the mat, arms straining with the weight of his offering.

It was a cumbersome machine, very black and very heavy. It smelled of grease. The young man breathed a grunt of relief as he set it down in the middle of the table.

"I've brought you some paper," he said, "and a couple of spare ribbons. They're in the car, I'll go and fetch them. Let me know how you get on."

He didn't stay – though Cath tried, Mabel couldn't be roused.

After she'd shown him to the door and closed it behind him, a churning in her stomach that might be excitement but was more likely disbelief, Cath realised she had most probably not said a proper thank you.

5

2021

"In fathoms of tumultuous wrath,

"In seething anger, plunging down . . .

"I can't remember any more of that masterpiece!" I tell my sister Joyce, "I just know I won the competition with it. After he brought me the typewriter."

"We'll get on to it," she replies – meaning her youngest daughter will. "We'll search the internet. You can find anything these days."

The editor wrote to me – or did I write to him? I can't remember. But he arranged to meet me. Joyce loaned me a skirt and blouse which would have been miles too big. I must have caught the bus into the city centre to the offices of *The Bristol Evening Post* and there I sat, across the desk from a man in a suit and tie with kind eyes. He told me how I might fulfil my ambition to become a journalist.

I was fifteen years old and hadn't been in school for nearly two years. Goodness only knows what I was wearing and what I looked like. I hadn't ventured out of the house for a haircut or to speak to anyone in the wider world since we'd moved in. I most probably couldn't string two sentences together.

"But look at you now!" says Sarah. "Writing a book!"

It's because two men – a social worker and a high-flying editor, whose names I don't recall – saw, and took the opportunity to show kindness. I'm reminded of Shirley's wisdom – no one is truly ordinary.

6

Bristol, 1st December 1969

Mabel was aware of being lifted onto a stretcher, felt the warmth of a heavy blanket, a strap being tightened across her middle; she heard a stranger's word of kindness close by her ear. Then the journey through the hallway where the naked bulb swung in the breeze from the open door, the jolt of the front step and the judder of her makeshift bed across the path, wheels rumbling on the concrete, the chill air of winter on her face.

It was dark – night perhaps; she passed under the glow of a street lamp and, for a moment, saw the profile of a man's face as he leant to adjust the pillow beneath her head. Then she was being lifted up, up into the soft light of a vehicle, the clatter of bolts beneath her, the slamming of doors, the thrum of an engine. It was all so very, very calm and peaceful. Only the painful rasping of her breath and the tightness of the strap which held her safe kept her from giving in to a blessed sleep.

Frank was sitting beside her, his face very close. She could feel his breath, warm on her cheek. He was holding her hand, which was a strange thing. She couldn't recall he had ever done that, in all the time they had been married. Perhaps, long ago, on a bench in Blagdon. Yes, perhaps then. Mabel endeavoured to turn her head but the effort was too much.

"Don't leave me, Mabe," she heard him say, softly. "Not after twenty-nine years."

Mabel shut her eyes tight against the sudden glare of an overhead light.

Epilogue

On the afternoon of 25th July 2021, Sarah, Joyce and I hosted an afternoon tea at Blagdon Village Club on the occasion of the anniversary, to the day, of Beatrice Mabel Howe's 100th birthday.

All the village was invited, and fifty-two people came. There was an abundance of bunting, criss-crossing the hall and caught up here and there with pink satin ribbon. Ten-year-old cousins were in charge of the ladder. Crisp white cloths were placed upon tables arranged in neat rows, floral napkins at every place setting. Baskets of pink roses and beautifully painted birthday cards to thank and welcome guests, designed and painted by the artist wife of my youngest son, graced each table. Vintage china from a hundred different Buckinghamshire charity shops displayed the nicest bakes and fancies, all from the local bakery. 1950s pop songs filled the airwaves and there was much chatter and laughter. A Blagdon lady with a love for music brought a keyboard and played wartime melodies. There was singing.

Shirley, a champion of every historic fact we have used to help us in our search for truth, displayed photographs of 1920s Blagdon on a board set upon an easel. We all shared the wonder of the Howe family portrait: Harry proud and tall, Lily seated so very elegantly with little Frances at her feet. A cameo of life before the scattering. A youthful Mabel smiled happily from the steps of Glebe House, and a 1930s school photograph had Jane and Mabel seated proudly in the front row, dresses neatly pressed and neck bows carefully tied.

The resident of present-day Glebe House sat amongst the guests and heard stories of times gone by, though no one knew the origin of the house name, and a lovely lady in a floral dress and black patent shoes took my hand and said our mothers had gone to school together.

A multitude of Howe grandchildren and great-grandchildren gathered, younger ones waiting on tables and pouring tea carefully into bone china cups, offering seconds when guests could drink no more but said "yes" anyway, because the children were so lovely.

It was a tea party for Mabel in the village where we have decided to believe she was happy. And in setting down these remembrances, searching for who our mother was and who she longed to become, it has brought a redemption of sorts. Sarah says that now our story has come to an end, she feels a sense of peace; that alone has made the journey worthwhile. Sisters together, always.

Acknowledgements

Grateful thanks to Dr Kathryn Heyman, my most excellent mentor and encourager, without whom this story would not have found its way onto a page.

Also my husband and family, for their unswerving belief that I could become a writer.

My daughter-in-law designed and gifted the glorious cover, so that Mabel's story might be nestled within the sweetness of a fragrant, everlasting bouquet.

And of course I must thank Sarah and Joyce, my fellow adventurers through life – the knowledge-keepers. They are anxious to thank me, their little sister, for writing these truths upon a page; for recalling how very hard Mabel tried. I may have been the scribe, but they have been the inspiration. Sisters together, always.

www.ingramcontent.com/pod-product-compliance
Lightning Source LLC
Chambersburg PA
CBHW062100080426
42734CB00012B/2699